BORIS JOHNSON is the me[...]
Henley-on-Thames. He is a jou......ust and author of
Lend Me Your Ears; Have I Got Views For You;
Friends, Voters, Countrymen; The Dream of Rome
and a novel, *Seventy-Two Virgins*. He lives with
his family in London and Oxfordshire.

Visit www.AuthorTracker.co.uk for exclusive
information on your favourite HarperCollins authors.

BORIS JOHNSON
LIFE IN THE FAST LANE
The Johnson Guide to Cars

HARPER PERENNIAL
London, New York, Toronto and Sydney

Harper Perennial
An imprint of HarperCollins*Publishers*
77–85 Fulham Palace Road,
Hammersmith, London W6 8JB

www.harperperennial.co.uk

First published in Great Britain by Harper Perennial 2007

1

Extract from 'The Garden Party' from *Complete Verse*
by Hilaire Belloc (Copyright © The Estate of Hilaire
Belloc 1970) is reproduced by permission of PFD
(www.pfd.co.uk) on behalf of the Estate of Hilaire Belloc.

A catalogue record for this book is
available from the British Library

ISBN-13: 978-0-00-726020-1
ISBN-10: 0-00-726020-2

Set in Helvetica by Rowland Phototypesetting Ltd,
Bury St Edmunds, Suffolk

Printed and bound in Great Britain by
Clays Ltd, St Ives plc

LIFE IN THE FAST LANE

CONTENTS

INTRODUCTION

For years after that terrible death, I felt a pang every time I pulled into Oxford station.

There was the scrapyard. There was the grabber with its evil jaws. Whenever I saw it I remembered the T-rex aggression with which it lurched down on its victim; how it paused and juddered as though savouring the moment.

Then it smashed through the windows, the windscreen, buckling the paper-thin steel, and with a hydraulic jerk the monster hoisted its prey. High in the air I saw it go, framed against the drizzly morning sky like some clapped-out old tup being lifted for the slaughter. I turned away because I could hear the whine of the crusher and I could not bear to watch the rest.

I could not listen to the death agonies of my driving companion, or see the reproachful look in those loyal headlights, and even today I cannot go past that knacker's yard without bidding peace to the ghost of the Italian Stallion.

It was the King of the Road. It was my trusty steed. It was a Fiat 128 two-door saloon, 1.2 litres, and a vehicle so prone to rust that it is years since I saw one in motion. In fact, the whole race of 1970s Fiat 128s seems to have oxidised into virtual extinction. They are fading as fast as the veterans of the First World War. You can hardly even find their photos on the Internet.

The Serbs kept making the 128 until the

1990s, under the brand name Zastava, until a crescendo of global ridicule reached a climax in 1999 when Bill Clinton and Tony Blair actually bombed the factory. Yes, Nato ended the production of my favourite car, as if those F-15s were charged with taking a surreal revenge on behalf of thousands of disappointed western consumers.

But from 1982 to 1986 it was the Italian Stallion, the machine that emancipated me from the shackles of childhood. Inside that happy brown plastic cabin, with its curious fungal growth on the roof, there took place all manner of brawls, romance, heartbreak and general growing-up. Above all, it was the car in which I had my first crash.

No one knew how the Italian Stallion came to be in the family. My mother claims it was hers, though other sources suggest my father bought if off a Brussels squash opponent called Sue.

It was sitting in the yard one day when my brother Leo and I decided to take it for a ride. Neither of us could drive, but there is a two-mile dirt track that links our farm to the main road, and we felt we could learn. We lolloped off down the drive, groaning in first gear, until at length we reached the main road at Larcombe Foot, where the machine stalled and a cloud of steam rose from the bonnet.

We had a problem. We had to turn round, and we couldn't go on the metalled road, since neither of us had a licence. There was a large-ish dirt patch, in which a normal driver would simply have done a neat three-pointer. But we hadn't done a turn before and we were aware of another car about 20 yards away. This obstacle was probably the only other vehicle within five square miles of this bit of underpopulated moorland.

With every manoeuvre we made, we seemed to arc ever closer to the other machine, as if sucked by some fatal magnet. Now our boot was just feet from its bonnet, and it was necessary to reverse.

I had never reversed a car before.

Sweating and cursing, I at last pushed the gear stick into the right position. I lifted my foot smartly off the clutch; one of the lovely features of the Stallion was that it had a very forgiving clutch. You could pull away in second, and quite easily change from first to fourth, and vice versa, usually by mistake.

The wheels spun in the dust and the car shot backwards, like a bolt slamming suddenly home, and with a smooth easy grace we thumped into the other car. Of course I was too amazed to brake, and what Leo and I remember is not just the sweet impact in the small of the back. We both remember the sense of exhilaration as we shunted the only other car in the district rapidly and deftly into a tree.

When the tinkling had stopped, Leo broke the silence and said, 'Hey, that was great', speaking for every human being who has ever experienced the thrill of the automobile – the joy of moving far faster than nature intended, by a process you barely understand, and yet somehow surviving.

When I became a motoring correspondent it wasn't just because I am a speed freak (though I am, a bit, in a terrified sort of way). It wasn't just because I wanted an endless series of beautiful machines for the weekend (though that is a factor, I have to admit). It was also because, at the risk of being pretentious – and why the hell not, eh? – I am interested in politics and society, and it has always seemed obvious to me that the car has not only made our modern landscape, it has been the biggest revolution since print, and the spread of the car, like the spread of literacy, has been a fantastic and unstoppable force for liberty and democracy.

It was the invention that defined and created the twentieth century. In the last hundred years the car has done more for human freedom, I venture to suggest, than the aeroplane, penicillin, the telephone and the contraceptive pill put together. Add in the ice cream Mars Bar, the computer, the trouser press, the television and the non-stick saucepan, and you still do not approach the revolutionary quality of the automobile.

When any invention has such power to promote individual freedom, the state is always driven to respond. The more widespread a liberty becomes, the more necessary it seems for government to regulate, trammel and constrain.

As I look back 25 years to my life with the Italian Stallion, I see that box-rumped old Fiat suffused with the golden glow of an age of comparative innocence, because in the subsequent decades our masters have decided to control our cars, and our lives, in ever more detail. They want to control how we drive and in what condition. They want to regulate what we do in our cars, where we park our cars, and now they want to tell us where we can drive, installing inboard computers to check up on us. We have got to the stage where you can be threatened with imprisonment for eating a sandwich at the wheel, for heaven's sake.

I confidently predict that it will not be long before each journey, each turning of the ignition, each firing of the cylinders, will be a matter for negotiation between the driver and the state, because these days your car is deemed to be much more than a threat to life and limb.

It was a Fiat 128 two-door saloon, 1.2 litres, that emancipated me from the shackles of childhood. Inside there took place all manner of brawls, romance, heartbreak and general growing-up. Above all, it was the car in which I had my first crash.

Oh yes: the internal combustion engine now stands accused of threatening the existence of life on earth. The charges are incredible, terrifying. If the scientists of the Stern Review are to be believed – and who dares contradict them? – then every thin

trail of exhaust that curls from your engine
is snaking up to heaven, where it is joining
the exhaust of billions of other machines,
and together these vapours have already
quilted a thick tea cosy of carbon dioxide
about the planet.

And with every second that great
transparent envelope of fumes is getting
thicker and thicker. Round the clock the
sun's rays are penetrating that integument
of pollution and, as with a greenhouse, the
light goes in and the heat stays put, so
every day the atmosphere gets hotter and
hotter, the winters shorter and more feeble,
Hyde Park in August is turned into a
parched dustbowl, and every time you drive
your kids to school another poor polar bear
gives a bewildered growl as he plops
through the melting floes. In fact our whole
future looks so ghastly and stifling that I find
myself loosening my tie and mopping my
brow as I write these words …

In this sweaty dystopia I foresee a time
when you will have to engage in carbon
offsetting every time you make a trip to
Waitrose. You will have to ring up
Environment Secretary David Miliband or
one of his officials to explain how you are
going to propitiate the wrathful sun god; and
whenever we get to drive our cars, the
government will insist that we plant a small
bush, or possibly sponsor an abattoir to kill
a cow, since it seems that cows are up
there with planes as emitters of greenhouse
gas.

The government will make us have little
inboard satellite devices – installed by the
state in attack-proof steel black boxes – to

verify that we have travelled no further than agreed, and that we have taken the shortest route, and that our engines have parped and puttered no more than their stipulated quota of carbon fart ... and ...

Aaargh ... Is it really going to be that bad?

I don't mean, is global warming really that bad? I mean, is the future of motoring so grim?

Will the state finally annihilate the joy of the car?

Or will Science come to the aid of Freedom – as she has so often in the past?

If we want to understand the future we must, as ever, look back. Going back in history, we can see reasons for gloom, and reasons for hope, and we can see that the state has always panicked in the face of any transport revolution. From the very introduction of the railways in the mid-nineteenth century, the ruling elite were nervous of mass mobility. All those people! Moving around! And under their own steam! In Disraeli's *Sybil* (1845) Lord de Mowbray warns against the railways for having a 'dangerous tendency to equality'.

As late as 1897 the pathetic male students of Cambridge protested against the arrival of female students; the trouble with these harpies was that they presumed to travel independently, and on complex pieces of machinery that they indelicately straddled, and which they could handle as well as a man. When they hung an effigy of a female undergraduate from a lamp post, it was significant that she was attached to that engine of sexual equality, the bicycle.

These alarms were nothing, of course, to

the shock that greeted the arrival of the first motor car. What happened to the first Benz machine upon arriving in London from the docks in 1894? What do you think? It was stopped by a policeman.

Before I start moaning about our namby-pamby, mollycoddled, airbagged society, I had better admit that those Victorians – those tough old Victorians, whose children died in droves, those Victorians who lived cheek by jowl with death and pestilence – were so terrified of the new motorised machines that they make the Royal Society for the Prevention of Accidents look positively gung-ho.

It really is true that during the first few years of the automobile's existence in the UK it was regulated by the Red Flag Act, originally designed for traction engines. This measure restricted speeds to four miles an hour in the country and two miles an hour in the town, and required every 'road locomotive' to have three attendants, one to walk no fewer than sixty yards in front carrying a red flag.

Admittedly, this insanity was soon repealed but it wasn't long before British MPs were engaged in their characteristic activity – whipping up public panic about some new threat to health and safety, then demanding legislation. By 1909 the car was still only about as powerful as a kind of motorised sewing machine, yet some Liberal MP was so wet as to stand up in parliament and warn the electorate about 'wandering machines, travelling at an incredible rate of speed' (i.e. 4mph).

Adumbrating one of the major themes for

'elf 'n' safety campaigners for the next hundred years, this Liberal went on to have a pop at drink-driving. 'You can see them on Sunday afternoon,' said the anti-car Isaiah, 'piled 20 or 30 feet deep outside the new popular inns, while their occupants regale themselves within.' Already, it seems, the car was associated with sin: unnatural speed, disrespect for the Sabbath and alcoholic intoxication!

His warnings were quite counter-productive, of course, since anybody listening to his speech would have been filled with an immediate desire to drive to the pub. Humanity fell on the car with greed and amazement.

It was as though, as a species, we had found the biggest technical improvement in our lives in a million years of evolution. By replacing the four legs of a horse with four rolling wheels we stumbled on something as important, and as naturally suited to human dimensions, and as obvious, in retrospect, as the shoe – or the wheel itself.

Between 1919 and 1939 the number of cars on the roads in Britain went up twenty times, with the millionth Morris rolling off the Cowley production lines shortly before the Second World War, and as the invention began to percolate down through the socio-economic groups, it began to democratise the planet. Until the First World War, it was a luxury item. As Hilaire Belloc puts it:

> The rich arrived in pairs
> And also in Rolls-Royces.
> They talked of their affairs
> In loud and strident voices.

But even as he wrote, a production breakthrough had taken place in America.

He went on to say:

> The poor arrived in Fords
> Whose features they resembled.
> They laughed to see so many lords
> And ladies all assembled.

And there we have it, in the merriment of those Ford-driving folk: the chirpy insolence of democracy. They knew that in spirit and in essence a Ford was the same as a Roller; though the rich man might still have his castle and the poor man might still be at his gate, they both possessed implements as essentially alike as one fork is like another, and although one fork may be of steel and one may be of gold, they will be equally suited to their task.

From the very beginning, rich and not-so-rich had basically the same set of four wheels propelled by the same internal combustion engine, and controlled by the same steering wheel, and above all we human beings found that the car created a great equality in our ability to occupy, at any one time, that rectangular patch of road beneath the chassis.

It is in the nature of the machine and the design of roads that we must wait in the same traffic and stop at the same lights, and it is significant that it was only in some of the worst left-wing tyrannies, such as the Soviet Union, that for part of the twentieth century the ruling elites had car lanes reserved for themselves. Everywhere else the car levelled and democratised the experience of motion, and it is no wonder that the spread of the car coincided with the spread of universal suffrage in the west and with female emancipation.

Even more completely than a bicycle, a car neutralises any female disadvantage in strength. It gives her a cabin, a door that locks, a place to put her stuff. It allows her to be Madame Bovary without having to worry about the discretion of the coachman, and in spite of all the efforts by the male sex to blacken their name, the overwhelming statistical evidence is that women drive better and more safely than men. They may fail their three-point turns, on average, more than male driving test candidates, but having passed, they have fewer accidents and attract far lower insurance premiums.

It is a sign of male desperation, and failure to adjust, that throughout the twentieth century we find deprecation of female driving skills – even from the finest stylists of English literature. One thinks of Evelyn Waugh and his ho-ho account of Mrs Stitch, bowling along the pavement in her glossy black machine until she ends up in a male urinal. Then note how two of the greatest American novels of the last century revolve around exactly the same sexist plot device – viz. *The Great Gatsby* by F. Scott Fitzgerald and *The Bonfire of the Vanities* by Tom Wolfe. Remember: in both cases a man takes the rap for a woman's fatal and incompetent driving. Isn't that typical, eh? Blame the woman.

Ever since Eve, ever since Pandora, the male sex has muttered the same essentially protectionist mantra, that the womenfolk can't be trusted with the technology, and if you seriously want to restrict the freedoms of the female sex and you seriously believe that modern western values are deplorable, then you actually continue to ban women from driving at all – as they do in Saudi Arabia, home of Osama bin Laden.

But for the British male and the American male and the rest of the western male sex, there was only one conclusion to be drawn from the sight of women at the wheel of a car. If you were going to let them drive, then you might as well let them vote as well, because apart from anything else, if you continued to deny the vote to female drivers, then the suffragettes would eventually stop hurling themselves under the hooves of horses and start running you down on street corners.

Yes, it was the car that made it impossible and ludicrous to deny women the political equality that had eluded them for 40,000 years, and for that achievement alone all remaining feminists should go outside now and reverentially kiss the hubcaps of the first automobile they see.

It was the car, too, that liberated the poor, that mobilised the Joad family in *The Grapes of Wrath*, that gave the victims of the Depression the chance to build a new life in California.

How did Herbert Hoover win the 1928 presidential election? With what vision did he inspire and enthuse the American electorate? He promised a 'chicken in every pot – and a car in every garage, to boot'.

And what was it, 60 years later, that finally brought down communism? It was a car. It wasn't just that the Ossies drove their Trabants round the Berlin Wall and through Hungary in such an unstoppable tide that in 1990 the East German state collapsed. The Trabant was not merely the instrument of revolution; it incarnated the point and necessity of the revolution.

It was a horrible two-stroke belcher of brown particulate smoke that would have rusted as fast as the Italian Stallion, except that its shell was made of a weird commie resin strengthened by wool or cotton. Its top speed was 112kph and it was a living sputtering embodiment of the economic humiliation of socialism.

It wasn't Ronald Reagan who won the Cold War. It wasn't

Margaret Thatcher. It was the daily misery of East Germans trying to get their Trabants to work, when they could turn on their televisions and see images of their West German counterparts and relatives roaring around in Golf GTIs. Yes, it was the car that spread capitalism and destroyed communism; no wonder Polish Pope John Paul II gave a Trabant a special blessing when he visited Sofia in 2002.

The car was at the centre of the most important events of the last century and was in many ways responsible for them; and still the motor revolution goes on because the number of cars is still growing, and growing fast.

When Leo and I crashed that Fiat in 1983, it was one of 18.6 million cars in the UK. Today there are 30.6 million registered cars. That's right: the number of cars on UK roads has almost doubled in the last 25 years, and there are still about half a million new registrations a year; when you consider how much longer a car lasts these days, you can see that the British people are adding to their stock of viable cars far faster than they are adding to the number of indigenous British people.

We have, in other words, a car population boom. We have a crisis in car demography that some believe is as serious as the boom in the number of pensioners and the change in the dependency ratio. We seem to have more cars than our roads can support.

When I was at Oxford, you could get to London in little more than an hour; these days the traffic can start at junction six of the M40. I remember once being stuck in the Italian Stallion – a car with all the torque of a bath chair – and realising that I had 18 minutes to get from the traffic lights at Hillingdon (as they were) to a vital job interview in Mayfair, yet somehow we did it, me and the Fiat, in broad daylight, in mid-morning, and in conformity with the laws of the road. And where did I park?

In the last hundred years the car has done more for human freedom, I venture to suggest, than the aeroplane, penicillin, the telephone and the contraceptive pill put together.

Right outside, of course: slap bang outside the headquarters of GEC, because those were the days before traffic wardens all became bonus-hungry maniacs and, although the Italian Stallion was already showing signs of the terrible wasting disease that finished it off, although it could only go up steep hills in reverse (reverse being for some reason the most powerful gear), and although by now a horrible green fluid leaked from the radiator, those were the days when it was still cool and rare for a student to own any kind of car at all, and I will always be grateful to Ken Livingstone and the Inner London Education Authority for the maximum grant that enabled me to

keep the Italian Stallion on the road,
because it made me one of a tiny minority,
and because I was one of a tiny minority I
would park it all over the place.

My favourite parking spot was on the
yellow lines by the squash courts in Jowett
Walk and sometimes, it is true, I got a
ticket. But what did I care? The Italian
Stallion had a James Bond feature that
enabled me to beat the fuzz. As a means of
eluding the law, it was far better than a
gadget that squirted the road with oil or tin-
tacks, or rear-firing cannon mounted by the
exhaust. The Stallion had Belgian plates.

What were the poor parkies going to do?
Contact Interpol? Ring up the Belgian
police and ask them to track down my
father's squash partner Sue? Ha. I snapped
my fingers at the parking tickets. I let them
pile in drifts against the windscreen until –
for these were the days before they were
even sheathed in plastic – the fines just
disintegrated in the rain.

Before you get stroppy, let me hasten to
say that I have more than made up for it
since. With the many thousands of pounds I
have paid to the parking enforcement
departments of Islington, Camden and
Oxfordshire, I wouldn't be surprised if I have
contributed enough, over the years, to pay
for a full-time teacher's salary, although if I
know Islington the cash has probably gone
on more traffic wardens, or the endless
abstract creation and destruction of road
humps.

There was an amazing optimism, in
those days, about parking, a prelapsarian
innocence, a belief that even on a double

yellow you would probably get away with it for an hour or so. It is with incredulity that I look back at my happy-go-lucky parking style – because even in that Elysium, in 1983, a terrible new plague had just come ashore.

It had been invented thirty years earlier by one Frank Marugg, a musician with the Denver Symphony Orchestra and a good friend of the sheriff, and it was designed to scare the pants off ticket-dodging swine like me. The first horrific sighting was in Pont Street, lovingly clamped round the wheel of a black Golf belonging to a record producer. From then on the yellow scourge spread like ragwort in our streets.

I remember in the mid-1980s rounding the corner of St James's, where the Stallion was as usual stationed in defiance of all bylaws, and when I saw that evil metal gin about its forequarters I felt a sudden constriction in the throat: a spasm of rage and amazement.

How could they do this? By what right could the state take away my freedom of movement? Except that it wasn't the state that had clamped my car, but a hireling of the state, a ruthless cowboy, and I was lucky compared to some.

In 25 years of tears, wails and ruined mornings, the clampers have immobilised a hearse with a corpse in the back, a Royal Mail van and a Good Samaritan who had stopped to help the victim of a hit-and-run driver. A disabled man of 82 was clamped in a pub car park because he walked out of the pub to post a letter before buying his usual half pint. The gangsters told him to pay £240 or see the fine increased even further. The other day they clamped the mayor of Middlesbrough while he opened a nursery.

If I sound bitter, it is because I am; yet the ruthlessness of the clampers is nothing next to the rapacity of their accomplices, the tow-truck operatives. An Englishman's car used to be his castle, or at least his mobile fort. I mean it was unthinkable that some public authority could simply move it. Yet time and again I would arrive at my *Spectator* office in Holborn, park the car, go in and ask my then assistant Ann Sindall for some cash to put in the meter, and while she was rustling around in the desk I would look out of the window and – blow me down! – there it would be: my car towed ignominiously past with its rear in the air, and without so much as a by-your-leave.

Which left me with that bleached-out beaten feeling you get when you have succumbed to the might of the state, and then in my dejection I would remember the logic of what they were doing and I would see the other side of the story.

I mentioned that cars were rare at university in 1983, even a Belgian-registered rust bucket. Nowadays students at Oxford Brookes University have so many cars that they park them all over the adjacent village of Holton, causing a grade A problem for yours truly, the local MP. You may wonder how students can afford so many cars, with the top-up fees and the debt and all. The answer is that car prices have risen very slowly, so cars are relatively cheap these days and more plentiful, with the result that the very person who spends his morning hurling oaths at a tow-truck operative may then recover his car and spend the afternoon in a traffic jam sobbing with incontinent rage because someone else has parked in a selfish place.

Cars make two-faced monsters of us all, and as the number of cars continues to rise, our hypocrisy will grow. More and more households have two or three cars, but then think of all the people in Liverpool or Manchester, where 48 per cent of the population still do *not* have a car. How will the government prove that they have been 'lifted out of poverty'? When they have a set of wheels, of course.

The more cars there are, the slower we all go, and although our machines are capable of ever more breakneck speeds, we are statistically less and less likely to break our necks. The current motorway speed limit is 70mph, which is a joke since the average – the *average* – speed on a motorway is 71mph, and 19 per cent of cars travel at more than 80mph. Yet in spite of the colossal increase in the number of these whizzing steel projectiles, the number of serious traffic accidents declined from 25,124 in 1992 to 18,728 in 2002 and the number of fatalities from 1,978 in 1992 to 1,795 in 1997.

If we keep going like this, in fact, we will reach levels of safety unheard of since the origins of the car. In 1914 there were only 132,015 cars on the road, compared to 30.6 million today. But in 1914 the total number of road fatalities – in England, not Flanders – was a stonking 1,328. What does that tell us? It tells us how much safer our cars have become.

Not that you'd ever guess, to judge by the way the Liberal Democrats of Islington go around installing these pyramids, these exhaust-scraping flat-top ziggurats, in the middle of the road. Sleeping policemen have multiplied 10 times in the last five years, says the AA. Across the country the ramps, pyramids and corrugations have become one of the divisive issues of our times: dividing communities, dividing us individually. We want them outside our houses to slow down the boy racers, but elsewhere we are fed up with driving as if through the badlands of Beirut. In 1983 we'd have thought it bizarre and decadent that the state should actually spend our money to make the roads worse. We never thought a government would be so Orwellian as to install the Gatsos, the oppressive wayside paparazzi, waiting to catch us driving in a compromising fashion and then – can you believe it? – actually threatening to send the grainy pictures to our home addresses unless we cough up.

The lobby groups love a new safety campaign, because a new safety campaign means an opportunity to raise new funds. The lawyers want new legislation, because new legislation means new grounds for litigation. The politicians are always hoping to identify themselves with some fresh measure to protect the electorate, so that they can imagine themselves as the new Gracchus or Disraeli or Shaftesbury. And the newspapers – well, the newspapers want to sell newspapers by warning their readers of some new terror and then demanding action.

In the face of this overwhelming pressure it is all but insane for anyone to object, even when the safety measure in question is manifestly pointless and anti-democratic. I will not now make a fuss about the ban on mobiles in cars, since I don't think I could win a statistical shoot-out with the 'elf 'n' safety boys. I merely point out that driving and telephoning does not seem to me to be fundamentally different from using your free hand to pick your nose, hit the children or turn the radio from Magic FM to something less glutinous.

Nor will I object to seat belts, since they plainly save lives, though my grandfather never wore one in his life, on the grounds (very reasonable, it seems) that they may induce a false sense of security, rather like cycle helmets. And I confess that the Johnson family has been pretty religious about the use of children's car seats.

But what about booster seats? I mean, stop me if you've heard me on this subject before, but what the hell is that all about? When we were children we didn't have car seats. We didn't even have seat belts. We bounced about in the back like peas in a rattle, and although our Renault 4 was a glorified vomitorium we all felt pretty happy and safe.

What happened to the first Benz machine upon arriving in London from the docks in 1894? What do you think? It was stopped by a policeman.

And now they tell us that if we have children under the age of 12, or four and a half feet in height, we all have to go to Halfords and lash out 30 quid on a plastic banquette booster seat, and we have to shove it under our children every time we go out in the car. I have done some research, and it is vanishingly improbable that you will make your children any safer with this device, yet the whole thing was cooked up in the dark by some EU transport official, rammed through parliament without any proper consultation. All it has achieved is the irritation of adults and the delivery of a serious blow to childish prestige.

The whole thing is mad, mad, mad, and shows, in my view, why important public servants like the police find it increasingly difficult to deliver the results we all want, and at the risk of being party-political, it demonstrates why we need a new approach to government in this country (cue Tory cheers, Labour groans, etc).

Before I am lynched by anxious parents, may I point out that all these safety measures can have perverse consequences, not least that they have made cars much heavier. We are all, myself included, much fatter than we were in 1983; in fact, 22 per cent of us are obese. The steel frames of our cars must therefore be ever chunkier and more rigid to carry our vast butts, and we also have six airbags and side impact protection systems and roll bars and crash frames and new extra-thick shatterproof glass, and not forgetting the extra buckles needed for those booster seats.

So our cars, like our people, are getting fatter and fatter. In 1991 a Honda Civic weighed 2,127 lbs; it now weighs 2,877 lbs. The little old Mini Cooper (pre-2000) weighed a mere 1,500 lbs, and the new one porks on to the scales at 2,314 lbs. The Golf GTI has been on such a binge diet of hi-cal safety devices that it has put on 234 lbs in the last five years. The result of this automotive obesity is of course a ludicrous circularity. The engines need extra sound-deadening equipment to hush the noise of the engines struggling with the burden of all that sound-deadening equipment.

Take, by contrast, the Fiat 128 Italian Stallion, a vehicle that did not afford the driver a notable sense of security. It had one seat belt, a long liquorice strap with no inertia reel, which you could wrap cosily around both driver and passenger, and which would do no good in a crash but would fool a policeman. You could push the car back and forth with one hand, and its entire body shell could probably have been composed of the same amount of steel that goes into one crumple-proof Mercedes bonnet. But if the occupants of the Fiat were aware that their machine was no tank, the occupants of other cars – and pedestrians – were at much less risk from the Stallion than they are at risk from its equivalents today.

If Leo and I had reversed at that speed in a modern car, there would have been a much louder thump and a much longer tinkle, and any occupants of the only other car in the district might even have had whiplash.

So we come to the eternal law of unintended consequences. By making cars safer, we seem to have made them more dangerous, yet no politician in his right mind is going to stand up and call for fewer safety features. No one is going to suggest that booster seats should be optional, though they plainly should be. So who is there left to speak for liberty?

Business? Industry? Don't make me laugh. Industry depends completely on regulation, because it makes the market, and for dominant firms it is always a good idea to encourage regulation that your smaller rivals will find expensive and difficult to obey.

The best and most hopeful thing we can say is that the human spirit is infinitely ingenious, and there will always be a struggle between the desire for individual freedom and the state's desire for control. The history of warfare teaches us that one technical advance will be met with a response. As the sword produced the shield, and the clamp produced the angle-grinder, so the speed camera produces the fuzzbuster and those handy cans of spray-on mud for the number plates, and the challenge of the Lib Dem road hump is met with the proliferation of mums driving colossal tractor-wheeled 4x4s through the streets of London.

Whatever new measures they come up with to punish the car for its carbon emissions – new taxes, journey restrictions, black boxes – I am completely confident that technology will supply the answer.

The scientists I meet tell me we really are on the brink of something miraculous, in the form of a working hydrogen fuel cell.

After more than a century of global dominance, the fossil fuel-based internal combustion engine is nearing the end. But not the car; oh no, the car will go on – but with exhaust fumes as sweet and inoffensive as a baby's breath and with a tread as silent as velvet.

And you and I will joyfully buy the wonderful new machines, clean and silent as snow.

And each with a red flag before them as a warning to the deaf.

In the meantime, it is my pleasure and privilege to introduce some of the finest, fastest and most fantastic machines on the road. It is an all-star line-up, assembled from across the globe, and though the car is now a cosmopolitan creation – like the honey in Waitrose – each marque still somehow breathes its national particularity.

We have the best of Germany, Japan, America, Italy, and as I flip down the list I am stunned to see how many British cars there are. It is a comment on our habit of national self-deprecation that you probably didn't even realise that Britain now has more independent car manufacturers than any other country on earth.

That's right: us, the Brits, the people whose technical know-how is supposed to be dying, and whose automobile industry was brought to its knees by Red Robbo and the Morris Marina and the Austin Allegro. It is astonishing to see how many British cars there are at the top end of the market, and how various they are.

The reader may sometimes wish that I hadn't anthropomorphised or hippomorphised or indeed gynaecomorphised these machines so often, but all I can say is that is how they felt to me at the time. They all have their specialities, and each has its virtues and fallibility.

I have done my best, anyway, to convey the enormous fun they have given me, and if my tone is now verging on the wistful it is because it is late April, and getting hotter and hotter. Soon the summer will be here, and the yammering terror of global warming will be on every front page.

In a few short years, I predict, these fossil-fuel-powered internal combustion engines will be museum pieces, and we will trace our hands down their motionless flanks with the reverence of those who love steam engines.

So here they are in their natural state – alive, wild, and still legally available. Feast your eyes while you can.

ROMEO IS SPEEDING

Being overtaken by a lady driver in a little car triggered a crisis of virility in our motoring writer. Luckily, help was at hand from Alfa Romeo's new 156 Selespeed.

She was blonde. She was beautiful. She was driving some poxy little Citroën or Peugeot thing with enormous speed and confidence. And she had just overtaken me on the inside of the A24 on the way to Dorking. And let me tell you, I wasn't having it.

Because if there is one thing calculated to make the testosterone sloosh in your ears like the echoing sea and the red mist of war descend over your eyes, it's being treated as though you were an old woman by a young woman. Especially when you are behind the wheel of an Alfa Romeo.

As I watched her rear waggle ahead of me, I quietly breathed the battle cry of the *Alfista*. My fingers found the electronic Selespeed gear buttons, positioned right there on the steering wheel like the buttons on a Formula One machine – or, indeed, like the zappers on an F-15E Strike Eagle, as used over Serbia to release the smart bombs and send them into Slobba's sock drawer – and *click*, my thumb depressed the left-hand button, marked with a minus sign.

And somewhere in front of me, in less than one and a half seconds, though I cannot vouch for the technical accuracy of the terms, the cormthrusters actuated the crabbing-pins. And, at precisely the moment I ordained, the machine changed down to third with the kind of throaty roar one might expect from a Turin stadium when Juventus equalise against Lazio.

'*Avanti!*' I hissed. '*Prestissimo!*' Then *click* with the thumb, down to second. The car howled out of the Leatherhead roundabout like a quark from a cyclotron and, with her bobbing number plate now in my sights, the whole endocrine orchestra said: 'Go. Take.' You can't be dissed by some blonde in a 305.

As I watched her rear waggle ahead of me, I quietly breathed the battle cry of the *Alfista*.

Yes, there is something about the very marque, Alfa, that makes the seminal vesicles writhe like a bag of ferrets. From the age of eight, when I made a model of some vintage machine, I have known that it stood for *Anonima Lombarda Fabbrica Automobili.* That great factory on the Padan

The electronic Selespeed gear buttons, positioned on the steering wheel like the buttons on a Formula One machine or the zappers on an F-15E Strike Eagle.

plain where hatchet-faced Italians tune, tune and tune the engines they love until they burble, like the cooing of sucking-doves outside your bedroom on a Tuscan hilltop as the morning sun strikes the honey-hued stone; or like the *blib blib blib* of Lavazza coffee gently ejaculating through the nozzle of an espresso machine. And it was then, no doubt, that I conceived my passion for the cars that have ruled my life.

There was the beautiful, red 33 Quadrifoglio 1.5, which went like a bomb until the left-hand headlamp connected with a meat-pie van on a Cornish B-road at 1am and the elegant rectangle of the chassis became a parallelogram. There was the silver GTV, whose porous engine block produced such a pall of brown smoke that you couldn't see out of the rear and Dutch police would arrest you for violating EU emission rules.

Finally there was the gorgeous, high, square-rumped Alfa 90 2.5 V6 *injectioné*: the kind of car in which Mafia dons were conveyed to meet Giulio Andreotti or Bettino Craxi in the good old days when the rust welled up beneath the paintwork of the Alfas like the great bubo of corruption beneath the skin of Italian politics.

As I think of that leal and trusty steed, I get all choked up remembering the day it died beneath me of a burst aorta on my way up the M1 to address a group of Tory activists in Llangollen. I was then forced to commandeer a taxi from Luton to North Wales at the cost of an average family holiday, arriving around 9pm to find my audience mutinous and pie-eyed on wine and cheese.

Seething, therefore, with those compound humiliations, I sought a kind of revenge in this the latest and most gizmo-encrusted Alfa 156 2-litre T Spark saloon; and you could feel the life-giving, baby's-brain-enhancing lead-free petrol surging hormonally into the cylinders, or possibly the carburettor, or wherever it's meant to surge. And soon that blonde was right back in front of my gorgeous, gouged-out snout, which looks a bit like a halloween lantern with a harelip.

And now we were coming into the Box Hill death run, where bonkers bikers yowl up and down from dawn till dusk on the dual carriageway. On any other day I would

Whether this blonde knew she'd been engaged in a test of a man's waning virility, I neither know nor care.

be tensed, white-knuckled in the slow lane, but today we were both giving those motorcyclists the humiliation they deserve, carving up the Kawasakis, and *arum arum arum araaaagh*, she took one and I took him too, our exhausts breathing contemptuously into his astonished face. Then we took another, and *araaagh* went the Alfa with the bubbling moan of lava in some volcanic pool of Etna, and now there was a clear stretch.

It was her or me. There was no excuse. There was no competition, not when the Selespeed contraption ensures that the interval in which you can move from third to fourth is tinier than the interval between a traffic light turning green on the Via Veneto and the man in the Fiat behind parping his horn, slapping on his door and shouting at you to move. Whether she saw me I do not know; and whether this blonde was aware that she had been engaged in a test of a man's waning virility I neither know nor care.

But I tell you this. My Alfa took her from behind, and I fairly thrummed it down into Dorking – 'Now you're Dorking,' I congratulated myself. And by making use of the high double-wishbone suspension system I was able to make a kind of genuflection to the speed limits, then round the cyclotronic roundabouts, and ho for Horsham and victory … Or so it should have been.

Perhaps it was complacency; perhaps I just forgot to look in the mirror. Whatever it was, we came to a roundabout a couple of miles later, and – *testa di cazzo!* – there she was, up there on my right shoulder as we came into the ring. She had the drop on me. She was pulling away and *plick* my thumb twitched reflexively on the Selespeed button to bring the engine down into first and turn the car into a monstrous uncorseted roaring of kinetic energy …

And *plick* I clicked again, *plick plick plick* and – *stronzo figlio di cazzo!* – the sodding thing stayed in second and there we were, wallowing on that roundabout, with as much élan as a piked porpoise. And as the tears started from my eyes, suburban Beemers flashed and honked, and her rump wiggled away for the last time …

Perhaps I might have caught up with her eventually, except that just then, without warning, my five-year-old child vomited all over the back seat, including the magnesium structure and submarining beam. Next time, give me a gear stick.

Vital statistics

Engine 2-litre, 16V
Top Speed 134mph
Acceleration 0–60mph in 8.6 secs
Mpg 33.2
Price (1999) £21,993

INHUMAN TRAFFIC

The war is over. Now all you have to do is get out of Kosovo in a Fiat Uno, without attracting the attention of the retreating Serb forces.

'**OK Vuk,**' I said to the cream-faced Serb as we nosed out of Pristina into bandit country, leaving the last Irish Guards Scimitar in the rear-view mirror of our Uno. 'Let's get the Vuk out of here.'

And let me tell you, that gibbering Serb needed no encouragement from me. Vuk was 29, with a head that tapered like an anvil from his rippling thorax. If I understood him correctly, he'd narrowly missed selection for the all-Serbia basketball team.

He could run a hundred metres in slightly over ten seconds. He didn't smoke. He drank nothing except Coca-Cola, to which he attributed properties of a barely credible order. Vuk was the kind of clean-living, God-fearing Serb that Arkan, the war criminal, used to recruit to his Tiger militia. In fact, it seemed Arkan had tried it on just the other day, at some rural wedding. When someone called Vuk a 'Serb maniac', he was delighted, flexing his muscles for days and saying, 'I am Serb maniac.'

Except that at this particular moment he was Vuk Funkovic, banjaxed with the terror of a man who knows that his people have done something very nasty, for a long time, to some other people ...

... But those other people had now got the upper hand, they'd got their AK-47s, and they were swarming all over the northern suburbs of Pristina, setting up illegal checkpoints on this dusty winding road, and winkling the fugitive Serbs from their Yugos and popping them like cringing molluscs; and there were 40 kilometres between us and the relative sanctuary of Serbia.

Which is why he was pedalling that throttle fortissimo and why, as I looked at the windows of his maroon Fiat Uno Testadicazzo 1.4 with bodywork about as bullet-resistant as a can of Diet Fanta, I said a little prayer.

Call me a sissy. Call me a wimp. But I felt the faintest frisson of apprehension to be driving through the retreating Serb army, past soldiers drunk on Slivovitz and hatred of Nato, when they had just shot three journalists on the suspicion (well-grounded, it turned out) that they were German.

As for Vuk: Vuk was *normally* brave. On the morning Nato came in from Skopje, and the other Serb drivers were cowering in the lobby of the glorified ashtray that is Pristina's Grand Hotel, saying 'I not go', it was Vuk who took me and Ivana, my gorgeous clean-living interpreter, down south to see the *joyeuse* entrée of the Gurkhas at the Kacanik pass.

Vuk had the guts to get out of the Uno and stand with me by the first mass grave the Paras found in Kosovo. He gulped but stood his ground when the black-bereted Albanian guerrilla appeared and started explaining how beneath the 89 numbered stakes where the flies buzzed, were the families that had been put in a tunnel, grenaded, and shot – shot by Serbs like Vuk.

He didn't mind when we flagged down a lurching Merc-ful of KLA, wizened gaffers in brown and yellow fatigues who flashed their gums and waved their Kalashnikovs like rattles. Neither Vuk nor Ivana showed the slightest fear of the American Rangers, backed up for miles in silence. They crouched behind their Humvees, guns trained, as motionless as the Iwo Jima memorial – apart from their rolling eyes and their trembling trigger fingers.

'What's up?' I asked one, tapping him on the shoulder. He pointed to the field, where the inky crows were flapping over the stooks and the poppies. It seemed someone had heard a shot. About half a mile away. You could tell the Americans had only just arrived.

Vuk even went to the headquarters of the KLA in Pristina, and he stuck it for a full 15 minutes while the youths in red armbands sidled up to him and asked him questions – first in Albanian, then more pointedly in Serbo-Croat. And now this self-styled Serb maniac was a pusillanimous pussy, and his hands were clenched on the clammy wheel in a kind of rigor mortis, and I found myself moaning, 'Not so fast.'

You soon understand the risks of driving in a war zone. Bombs? Phooey. I'd been bombed in late May, a couple of hours after arriving in Serbia, while driving down the deserted highway through Vojvodin. *Wump wump wump wump* went the precision munitions 300 yards away on our left, and the clouds wagged to heaven.

As I looked at the windows of his maroon Fiat Uno Testadicazzo 1.4 with bodywork about as bullet-resistant as a can of Diet Fanta, I said a little prayer.

Guns? OK, there had been one Pinter-esque pause when some Serb soldiers found out I represented the *Daily Telegraph*; and it was certainly my habit, going through the bosky bits, to balance my A4 Niceday pad on my head and cower behind the dashboard.

But the real risk was, of course, a car crash. 'I very good driver. You see,' said Vuk that morning we left Belgrade for Kosovo, in our *Wacky Races*-convoy of hacks. 'This very good car,' he said, showing off the Uno's finer features: its ability to carry five jerrycans of petrol; the way it could accelerate in fifth.

Just to prove the Uno's durability, he then reversed without looking and *wham*, our necks whipped as he crunched the bonnet behind us, a Golf belonging to Reuters. Luckily we sustained nothing more serious than a slightly squeaking door, which Vuk cured by anointing it with Coca-Cola, the drink he swore by and which expressed his rejection of Milosevic.

That is why I wasn't so fussed by the sight of the burning houses, or the sad-eyed Serb soldiers, or the KLA sharpshooters. We smiled and waved at everyone indiscriminately, and, alarmingly, they waved and smiled back – the Serbs assuming that Vuk was a Serb heading home, and the Albanians spotting a western journalist.

'This very good car,' he said, showing off the Uno's finer features: its ability to carry five jerrycans of petrol; the way it could accelerate in fifth.

No, what freaked me out were the signs of previous crashes – one car flattened like a can; that's what happens when you hit a T-55 – and trying to remember my blood group. With each fresh horror Vuk put his foot down harder, and cee-ripes, my fingers bit into the attractive leatherette Uno upholstery.

'Jesus H Christos,' I was murmuring when, with a rubber wail, the Uno stopped. '*Srbija!*' shouted the Serb, and poured himself a joyous libation of Coke. So we went on, bathed with relief, until a couple of miles on he spotted one of those purple-pyjama'd military policemen – the real bastards of the Kosovo purges – lounging unshaven by the road.

He waved us down. 'What the hell are you doing?' I whispered to Vuk. 'Don't stop!' Too late. The Serb maniac grinned as that unshaven, flat-eyed gunman got in the Uno's spacious rear seat, and stuck his Kalashnikov near my left ear, and I did my routine of pretending to be Boris Jonsson of *Svenska Dagbladet* for a couple of miles. 'It was your turn to be afraid,' said Vuk, as the militiaman got out.

As for the Uno, it's just the job for Kosovo; particularly if, like Vuk, you're smart enough to carry Czech plates.

Vital statistics

Engine 1116cc, 4 cylinders, 58bhp
Top Speed 92mph
Acceleration 0–60mph in 17.9 secs
Price (1999) £150

DUDE TALKS LIKE A LADY

Lexus have pitched the IS200 against the luxury car big boys. So why have they given it the voice of a girl?

Come on, baby, I say tersely to the girl, speak to me for heaven's sake. You know how it is when you're relying on some chick to map-read and they go all silent and sulky? We are coming down New North Road and some key decisions are in prospect. I'm not getting the help I need so I give Carol a poke with my index finger, because that's the kind of relationship we have.

Come on, darling, we're dawdling here in the middle of the road and there's a gravel truck behind us that wants urgently to deliver its gravel. Is it right or left? And I jab her again, harder, because that's the sort of guy I am, and then Carol speaks: so cool, so low, so scrotum-tighteningly thoughtful.

'In a quarter of a mile,' she says, 'turn right.'

Ah, don't you love her? She's somewhere in her early thirties and her voice is perfectly pitched to mesh, to blend, above all not to offend the turbulent emotions of a guy lost in the sweltering Palio of the London traffic.

They've done tests on your average, red-blooded, Lexus-buying British male, and they've found that he's a tricky customer. Give him a man's voice telling him what to do – some jerk with a plummy accent – when he's trying to do a U-turn in the middle of the Strand, or tax him with some toffee-nosed git correcting his choice of route, and what does he do? Under laboratory conditions your red-blooded, Lexus-buying male feels the veins in his neck become so engorged with incontinent rage that his collar button pops and, *pow!* He lets it all out with one savage blow of his left fist.

Crunch. Tinkle. Voice silent. Which is a pity, since Carol is the cleverest thing on four wheels. For a paltry £2,100 extra your

The Lexus IS200, fitted with a GPS satellite guidance system, a gizmo of mind-bending sophistication.

IS200 Lexus is fitted with a GPS satellite guidance system, a gizmo of such mind-bending sophistication that to see her for the first time is to feel like a South Sea Islander seeing his first aeroplane, or stout Cortez gazing at the Pacific. Imagine a talking A–Z, bashfully unfurling herself on the dashboard every time you turn the ignition. Imagine maps, gorgeous colourful maps of every corner of the British Isles, with the one-way streets helpfully marked out.

Carol's perfectly pitched to mesh, to blend, above all not to offend the turbulent emotions of a guy lost in the sweltering Palio of the London traffic.

Then imagine your route illuminated by a thick blue line, every revolution of your wheels transmitted – *ping* – to a satellite transponder, and *ping*, somewhere in the inky wastes of the heavens a throbbing nose-cone breaks off from transmitting Rupert Murdoch's ball-by-ball pornography to the people of Zimbabwe and tells your car there are exactly 150 yards to go before a right turn on the New North Road. Yes, that's you, that blue line inching down that street before your eyes, and you gaze in rapture until – 'Whoa, sorry old fruit, didn't see you there,' you say to the weaving, terrified cyclist.

Ahem: that is one disadvantage – the display doesn't show what else is on your street, and until all vehicles and pedestrians have their own satellite link-ups and we can drive about on instruments only, it is as well not to ignore that amazing technological breakthrough – the transparent windscreen. 'Whoa there', I say to the cyclist, but thanks to the sensational disc brakes of the Lexus he is unharmed, and shakes his fist in friendly greeting.

'In 50 yards …' says Carol, and I think how much I love that use of yards; yes, she's an imperial measurements sort of girl, Carol – strait-laced but sensuous, firm but tender, like an NHS nurse brusquely fluffing your pillows and then leaning over to take your temperature in fahrenheit, the watch pinned on to her snowy bosom, her ample bosoms … 'In 50 yards,' says Carol, 'right turn.' And then I think, wait a mo …

Hang on, girlie. What do you mean 'right turn'? How do you know that? This route is, I confess, well-known to me, since after working late in the evening I occasionally catch a cab home. This infrequent habit (expenses department, please note) taught me that to get from Islington to Canary Wharf it is cheapest and quickest to go via Commercial Road, though if you look at the map it appears that you go by Hackney. It costs roughly £11 to go my route, and it costs £14 to go the route the cabbies instinctively set out on.

Now, you would have thought that Carol could merely compute the shortest distance between two points; you'd have thought that like the cabbies, she'd ignore the traffic lights, the mini-roundabouts, the sleeping policemen and go via Hackney, even though it is slower. But no! I think she understands. I think she knows. Farewell A–Zs, you useless maps with the key page always torn out: may you rot in the boot in a compote of baby yoghurt and engine oil. Goodbye all you cabbies who boast of 'The Knowledge'. Adieu to the time-honoured pelmanism of black-cab drivers, the weeks they spend on bicycles committing the streets of London to their memory: what a devastating rebuke Carol has delivered to their chauvinism.

Farewell A–Zs, you useless maps. Goodbye all you cabbies who boast of 'The Knowledge'.

She doesn't raise her voice; she doesn't hit you with the map; and even if you accidentally hit her with your left hand and turn her off, she soon comes back to life and, with geisha-like deference, excogitates your next move. 'In half a mile, turn right. Shortly after that, turn left,' she says. Yes, you ask yourself, was there ever a girl so easy to turn on? 'Keep left,' she is saying as we come towards Spitalfields, 'keep left.'

In fact, there are three forks here. 'Keep left', says Carol again, as obstinately as a guide in the old Soviet Union, with brown stockings and suspenders. Now this time, I think, she's pushing me too far. She can't be serious.

But such is her prestige by now, so insistent is her voice, that I do as she says. I keep left, and we end up in a one-way system in Hoxton market.

A rubbish van is very slowly loading up. We are stranded outside the Aquarius nightclub and on the beer-splashed pavement, where the morning rays are starting to bring out the best of last night's vomit, the tough eggs are looking appraisingly at Carol and me. Get us out of this one then, Carol, I say; and maybe there was something sneery in my voice, because after that she never quite recovered her form.

We do eventually make it to Canary Wharf, after I scrape an alloy hub (sorry folks) in Hoxton. But as soon as we approach the Tower of Doom, she says, 'Do a U-turn as soon as possible.' I swear. That's exactly what she says. 'Do a U-turn as soon as possible.' Isn't that spooky? What does she know? And who can say she does not have my best interests in her lonely metal heart?

Vital statistics

In May 1999, the IS200 was launched against the BMW 3 series, Audi A4 and C-Class Mercedes.

Engine 2-litre, 250bhp 6-cylinder with 6-speed manual gearbox
Top speed 134mph
Acceleration 0–60mph in 9.5 secs
Price (1999) from £20,500

LITTLE
AND LARGE

Big Boris and the small Smart car made a great double act ... well, his builders and the Camden clampers thought they were a funny pair

You know, that Smart car could not have turned up at a better time, tactically speaking. The kitchen had no floor and wiring dangled pathetically from the walls where the stove and other vital appliances awaited installation. In our supposedly wonderful new sitting-room the fireplaces were gashes in the wall, from where there leaked increasing quantities of black dust which made the children cough. Every morning, about a dozen builders would turn up, spread their tins of dhal, chapati and okra across the lunar surface of the floor, and then begin an interminable, ruminative feast.

'Smart?' I spat. 'What's so smart about a machine you can't turn on?'

'How much longer?' we begged Bishi, the foreman with fascinating holes in the gristly parts of his ears. 'How long?' we wheezed with plaster-coated lungs, two weeks after the deadline had elapsed.

And Bishi the builder would grin, scratch his perforated ears and announce that, 'Brickie has not turned up!' And as for the skein of tangled pipes that presently served as the bathroom, it all depended on the plumber. Where was the plumber? 'Plumber is thinking,' said the foreman, and invited us to imagine his colleague cross-legged at home, meditating on the precise angle of the overflow.

One dark hour before dawn, shivering

under the duvet, I suddenly grasped the game of Bishi and Co. What was it about this sadistic go-slow? They doubted me, that's what it was.

They looked at me and saw a mere hack, a drudge who churns out articles by hand – a manual labourer! With their keen sense of caste, of hierarchy, they doubted – entirely reasonably, I may say – that I would be good for the final £30,000. And that was why they passed the brinjal pickle and delayed the completion of our brushed-concrete kitchen floor; and that was why they had put off finishing the patio. They wanted to see the colour of my money!

The cheek! Of course we had the money. It was just a flow thing. The dosh was backed up in some blocked U-bend in Barclays, Reading, waiting for a touch of the spanner from my Premier Service personal banker who, like the plumber, was presumably 'thinking'.

All I needed, it hit me, was a sign; a concrete and eloquent testimony to my wealth and station in life.

And that very morning, just as Bishi and Co arrived, a liveried *huissier* from the offices of Smart Car UK was to be seen in our street. 'Acha!' they exclaimed, as they drank in the glossy cuboid with all the rapt attention of the crowd on the Bombay maidan when Pakistan have six to win and an over in hand.

'It is a Mercedes!' moaned Bishi. 'Mercedes!' hissed the number two man. And as the word was passed down the line to the Painter, Tile Man, Concrete Mixer, Plumber (for it was he) and Brickie (he, too), I could feel my stock rising by the second, like some air conditioning company on the Delhi Bourse.

Quite forgetting their hectic timetable, the builders stayed to watch; if only to satisfy themselves that the machine was really mine.

Expertly locating the door handle among the eezigrip Swatch-designed panels – which can be mixed and matched from a range of upbeat pastel tones – I got in. Soon the admiring faces of the builders were lost to view. Not that the car had moved anywhere. The windows, though, were slightly steaming up as I tried and tried to find the ignition. Through the mist of the glorified goldfish bowl I could now sense that they knew this was not my car.

'Smart?' I spat, jabbing the key at every orifice in the fascia.

'What's so smart about a machine you can't even turn on?' The central concept of Smart, according to the bumf, is 'simplicity'. At Mercedes HQ in Dortmund, logicians with high, papery foreheads and lozenge-shaped spectacles have, in a fit of Freudian ecstasy, taken Car back to its infancy. The result is that everything is chunky and rounded in easy-wipe, vomit-resistant Fisher-Price plastic.

At the very best, this is either a Kiddikar or a girlie car. It would be absolutely fine, I was thinking, if you were an It girl with a brace of topiary-tailed poodles in the back seat – or if you were proposing to drive it accidentally-on-purpose into Prince William's South of France swimming pool.

In fact, I seem to remember Peter Purves driving just such a car in my 1974 *Blue Peter Annual*. He drove it to Paris and I have it in my head that he parked it sideways on the Champs-Elysées – exactly the sort of stunt the Smart can pull. And here I was, a quarter of a century later, the Peter Purves of *GQ* magazine, and I couldn't turn the bloody thing on.

Until at once, with a savage downwards jab at the key like a bad-tempered two-year-old, I accidentally found the right hole; by the handbrake for some reason ('*Natürlich, Gottlob!* What is starting but the opposite of stopping?') and *vroom!*

A colleague from *GQ* believes the car is like a motorbike with four wheels. 'There is nothing that can beat it away from the lights,' he says. That must depend, I think, on who is at the controls. I do not think that I would have been beaten by an old woman

Vital statistics

The Smart Car was launched in 1998 as the ultimate city runabout.

Engine 600cc, 6-speed manual gearbox, 3 cylinders
Top speed 87mph
Acceleration 0–40mph in 6.5 secs
Price (1999) from £8,499

in a bath chair as we kangarooed away from the lights on Liverpool Road. But you should not rule it out.

Once I'd sussed out the PlayStation-style, automatic six-speed gearbox, a vague sense of fun started to take over. I cannot

Everything in the Mercedes is chunky and rounded, in easy-wipe, vomit-resistant Fisher-Price plastic.

pretend that I tested my colleague's assertion that it can reach 90mph, certainly not on the route between Islington and the *Spectator*'s offices in Holborn. But if, like me, you rather like left-hand drive, and believe that the so-called motoring authorities encourage an aversion in the hope of deterring the ripped-off British public from buying cheaper cars from the continent; and if you think you might rather enjoy weaving around in a souped-up 600cc beer crate, then you might be a Smart kind of guy or gal.

You might enjoy squeezing its rump into a space no larger than a bath mat; though I should warn you that its charm has not yet penetrated the traffic wardens of Camden. First they clamped it. Then they just removed it – gone; tossed, perhaps, like a Dinky toy into some municipal cupboard.

There's no car smart enough to get itself out of that one. When I got home, on foot, Bishi and Co were tactful enough not to bring the matter up.

ALL ABOARD THE SKYLINE

Nothing can spoil Boris' enjoyment of the bionic new Nissan, not even a government apparently intent on taking all the fun out of driving.

There I was at some traffic lights on the North Circular, trying to work out the controls, when a shadow fell across my right shoulder and a voice spoke with the sarcastic respectfulness we all know so well. 'Evening, sir,' said the fuzz on his bike. 'Nice car you have there. Your fog lamps are on.'

So *that* was the significance of that little orange light. Could it be this knob? That knob? Twiddle twiddle. The fog lamps remained on. 'Do be careful, sir,' he said as the lights turned green. 'It can go very fast.'

'Absolutely', I called out. At this point I must have touched the throttle of my brand-new Nissan Skyline GT-R because that officer of the law suddenly vanished behind me, and it was ho for St Albans and a crucial meeting of that magnificent body of men and women, the Hertsmere Conservative Association. I wanged her round the flyover and then up on to the M1 and *arum-arum-arum*, I was just about to let the wild animal out of its cage and put it through its paces when I remembered the warnings of plod.

If I believe what I read in the papers – and of course I do – the boys in blue have decided that they have a new mission in life, which is to persecute and fine the middle-class motorist. And since there was no point in being delayed in police custody, I allowed them to dawdle – those great, fat, two-foot wheels, those Bridgestone radials with the Formula One silhouette, spitting gravel sideways as some great predator might spit the masticated, bony fragments of a deer.

According to the *Knight Rider*-style in-car computer gizmo, we were only using about 10 per cent of the throttle; and as for something called 'Boost', there was a whole lot of boosting this car wanted to do. But no, I said to the car. No boy, keep control of yourself there, as it reached the national speed limit in second or third gear (the gears remained a slight mystery) with barely 3,000 revs, its cardiac system as honed and superfit as Bruce Lee, its prowling haunches bulging with suppressed kinetic energy.

Whoa there, boy, I muttered, fingers clamped and clenched. We can't let the Tory party down. And though I say it myself, we didn't. I gave them hell, those Hertsmere Tories. I raved about the iniquity of Labour petrol taxes, the astounding fact that after we spent three months bombing to smithereens the Serb refineries, the gas stations, the tankers – fuel is still cheaper in the former Yugoslavia than it is in London.

'I tell you this, Mr Chairman, ladies and gentleman,' I continued amid tumultuous applause, 'there are now some garages where they offer you a free car every time you fill your tank!' Hear hear. Har har haaaargh. So it was in a fairly elated mood, you may divine, that I pressed the little remote-control key-unlocker type thing after supper, and the orange indicator lights blinked obediently.

As my foot pressed down, the car surged ahead like a stallion stung by a bee.

Now, let me say immediately that though I may have sipped a glass of Rioja, I was in full possession of my faculties. It was just that the mind turned inevitably to the questions of ideology we had recently been discussing. In the intensifying tyranny of Blair's Britain, where speed cameras pop at every corner; where Prescott and the police are about – it says here – to cut the speed limit to 60mph; isn't there a case, I thought, as the M1 uncoiled itself before me, eerie in the yellow sodium lights and all but empty, for some sort of gesture?

Isn't it only fitting that we defenders of individual liberty should match our words with deeds? Hardly had the thought formed when my foot pressed down and, *yeeeow!* the blue streak of tin-plated testosterone surged ahead like some stallion stung in the bum by a bee, and that monster cardiovascular system started to suck more petrol into its great, pulsating aorta, while the others cars were left behind as if they were bollards.

Luton is a lovely place, but never have man and machine passed it by with such scalding indifference. And as the needle crept into the three-figure mark, my doubts began. No, cried the voice of conscience. You have four children. Forget all this libertarian nonsense. Of course other people are affected by your actions.

It may be true that if you did a Henri Paul and hit the pillar of the motorway bridge, it would be you, and you alone, they would have to scrape off the tarmac with a teaspoon. But think of your family, think of your responsibilities, think of the poor chap who has to wield the teaspoon.

Slowly the foot came off the throttle like some postcoital detumescence, until I noticed that everyone else was now whizzing past my ears. They were howling past at 90,100, the Mercs, the Jags and even the little Fords, for heaven's sake. This was mockery. It was insupportable; and so I started that old game of preparing lines for the cops.

I could try the German tourist routine: '*Was ist los? Vot? Kann Man nicht in England schnell fahren?*' I could pretend to think that Euro speed limits had all been harmonised upwards to infinity, or that I was still on the road from Stuttgart to

Mannheim. Or maybe I should blub and point out that in all honour I had no choice.

'What can I say, officer? They made me. They're ruthless, these *GQ* people. If I write a column and they sense I haven't properly tested the car, I don't get paid, and if I don't get paid I can't – choke, sob – buy my children Fruit Loops for their breakfast ...'

First you notice you are travelling faster, then you feel as if your buttocks have been clamped by the leather seat.

And I pushed my foot down again ... and *zow*. There are two stages in this machine's acceleration. First you notice that you are travelling appreciably faster. Then you feel as if your buttocks have been suddenly clamped by the leather seat. And I may be wrong but I had the impression that my face was being pushed back into a gibbering rictus as the G-forces kicked in, and the stars turned into trails of light like a slow-release photo or the bit in *Star Wars* when they enter hyperspace. Or perhaps those weren't stars, they were road lights, but I was too terrified to flick my eyeballs to the left or right to find out.

We were now doing 125mph, which is the fastest I have ever been on land under my own propulsion, and I was just about to give it a breather when I remembered the words of my *GQ* editor, that this was a 'muscle car'. 'Muscle,' I grunted. And, for an instant, I took that machine up to 130mph.

And maybe that's nothing to you *GQ* boys, who have to wear clothes pegs on your noses to keep the virile hormones sloshing out of your nostrils, but it left me feeling, for a moment or two, like a man who had slipped the bonds of civilisation and rediscovered his bestial soul – and also, of course, like a bit of a prat. Officer, I promise I won't do it again.

Vital statistics

Originally launched in 1997, the new-look GT-R was released in October to take on the Porsche 911.

Engine 2.6-litre, 277bhp, 6-cylinder, 5-speed gearbox
Top speed 155mph
Acceleration 0–60mph in 4.9 secs
Price (1999) £54,000

BENTLEY DOES IT

So many people took so much care to make the Arnage Red Label the car it is: unfortunately for him, Boris ends up with nothing to chauffeur it.

I have a routine now with these cars from *GQ*. The trouble with being an ace car reviewer like me is no matter how expert you are in thrust and torque, there is one technical difficulty you can't easily overcome. These cars have no resident's permit. After a while, the parking tickets start to build up like drifting snow on the windshield.

Word was coming back from Morgan, *GQ*'s car overlord, that the chicks in the expenses department were starting to get antsy. And then I had two cars in a row towed. First I made the mistake of thinking that I, as editor of the *Spectator*, would have access to the *Spectator* garage. Oh no. That privilege goes to Kimberly Fortier, the magazine's publisher. And so one day I was on the phone to an agitated Norman Lamont, chewing the fat about Pinochet, as one does, when I looked out of the corner of my eye and saw the latest Jap supercar being hoisted through the air, which would have been fine except that I had let the same thing happen to a Swatch Smart Car the previous month.

The chicks in the *GQ* expenses department – and if you can't call them chicks, then what the hell, I ask you, is the point of writing for *GQ*? – decided to put their perfectly formed feet down. I had to find a garage. So that is how I came to be at the wheel of the most expensive car I have ever seen, inching with much squealing of new rubber around a cramped underground car park somewhere in Bloomsbury.

This Bentley Arnage Red Label is yours for £150,000, and it is huge. Its prow seems to stick out like a supertanker, its rump like a steel wedding dress. It has a radar gizmo which beeps as soon as its pristine grey flanks come too near another object – rather like a heart machine on a dying patient, or a Sidewinder missile locking on to its target: bip bip bip beep beep beeeeeep, and when it flatlines, you know the paintwork is only inches away from being scratched. And if, like me, you have by now developed a proper respect for the *GQ* expenses department, the sweat is starting to bead on your brow.

After about half an hour of trying to thread this mastodon through the eye of a needle, I was stuck. If I went an inch forward the machine beeped me, and if I went backwards, ditto. Every option seemed to involve a crunch and a tinkle. And then, as luck would have it, a very nice man appeared from nowhere and offered to park the thing for me. Now you might pause before handing a complete stranger the keys to a car worth as much as a castle in Scotland, a French chateau, or a garage in Notting Hill, but not this correspondent. 'Good on ye, mate,' I gasped to the chap as he smiled and cockily spun the wheel, calculating the angles like a snooker player, and the wing mirrors of the Bentley wagged like the ears of an obedient mastiff as he engaged reverse.

I suppose I could have tried some apologetic gag about how it was my chauffeur's day off, but I was actually too wrung out, trembling like a man rescued from a rock face when he has spent an hour unable to move up or down. Anyway, if Bentley are mad enough to lend the car to me they can hardly object – and their insurance premiums will hardly be affected – if I hand it over to someone who can actually drive it.

And when I came back in the evening, do you suppose my friend had made off with it? You have too little faith in human nature. Bagging the keys from Cyril the attendant, who must believe I am a man of serious substance to judge by the cars I have been leaving in his care, I pressed the remote-control gizmo to open the door.

For nigh on a century the craftsmen at Crewe have laboured to produce the last word in personal locomotion. From generation to generation have been transmitted the arts of hand-stitching the oxblood upholstery and anointing every seat with a pint of germolene until it is as soft and yielding to the buttocks as a pair of old Viyella pyjamas. From father to son has been passed the secret of buffing up the walnut burr; buffing and buffing with such a masturbatory frenzy that after decades of experiment the interior glows as radiantly as the half-parted lips of Joan Collins. The

From father to son has been passed the secret of buffing up the walnut burr ...

boffins at Cosworth have souped up the 400bhp six-and-three-quarter-litre engine, souping and souping until it is a gigantic minestrone of valves and tubes with more torque than any other saloon in the world.

This is the car before us now, the Bentley Red Label Arnage, and you can't even open it up. I press the tit on the key again. Zilch. The indicators wink, but the driver's door won't open. Entering by the passenger door, I set off the alarm, which fills the chambers of my skull like throbbing glue. I sit there, pushing every button I can find, until I am rescued by two charming blonde women on the way to a party.

'Arnage,' I mutter under my breath. 'What is this Arnage?' The word does not exist in English. It must be a mixture of 'carnage' and '*arnaque*', which is the French for 'a swindle'. Now it won't even let me move. The boys at Bentley have found somewhere so discreet, so tactful to hide the handbrake – that embarrassingly ordinary object – that Sir cannot find it. He cannot. Where in the name of holy f*** is the handbrake?

I pull the silver knobs on the fascia. I jerk bits of the seat this way and that. I yank the ashtray, the mobile phone holder, the air conditioning. It is now 25 minutes since I first tried to activate this *ne plus ultra* of comfort and convenience, I hope you won't be too shocked if I say that I start, in the gentlest possible way, to freak out. That doesn't work either.

It is now after 8pm and all the honchos at *GQ*, Rolls, Bentley, etc will have knocked off. Then inspiration strikes. I use my mobile phone to contact the Bentley dealership in North America, whose number is on the press pack at my feet. 'This is Hamish McSquatter,' says an answerphone somewhere. As I bounce up and down, howling, on the coach-built upholstery, I reflect that this car has every accessory but one: someone in a peaked cap to drive the damn thing.

Vital statistics

The Arnage Red Label will compete with the most prestigious cars around. Nearest rivals are the Mercedes S500 and BMW 740i.

Engine V12, 24-valve, 6.75 litre
Top speed 140mph
Acceleration 0–60mph in 3.5 secs
Price (2000) £149,000

HOME IN THE

RANGE

Boris has his ups and downs in the new Range Rover Autobiography but thankfully his story does have a happy ending.

Do you want to know the honest truth about Range Rovers? Do you want to know what I think of them? Well, as a general rule I had thought that they were for poseurs, ponces and pseuds, and anyone who wants to delude himself that he is the hero for an advertisement for malt whisky, or an off-duty diamond prospector from the pages of Wilbur Smith.

Those dirty great wheels with their 50cm wading depth, what did they ever do but mince around the lawns of Glyndebourne or carry boy-racers across Hackney's tarmac wastes? Do you know who buys the Range Rover? The Italian upper classes. Calling it a 'Rainch', they bomb up and down the autostrada, pushing its vast muzzle into each other's rumps at 100mph – their signal that they would like to overtake.

'What's the difference between a hedgehog and a Range Rover?' someone asked me when I was about ten, and appreciated that kind of joke. With a Range Rover, the pricks are all on the inside. Gah, we used to say when we were children. Huh, we used to say when we passed a Range Rover on the motorway; because when we were nippers, we had a Land

Rover. And a Land Rover was proper.

Our Land Rover was so beaten up that its roof had been wrenched away by a tree. Its door fell off when you opened it. Its ignition was operated by a twig tied on with baler twine. And when you started it thick, delicious grey clouds of diesel smoke would fill the nostrils and it throbbed and vibrated like the climactic scene in an equestrian novel by Jilly Cooper. After 25 years of being rained on, snowed on and pushed by a cow – I kid you not, just ask whichever of my siblings had left the handbrake off – down a hill and knocked upside down into a ditch, that triumph of British industrial design would still take you up the most savage inclines Exmoor had to offer.

I experienced the adulation accorded to those who own a machine like this.

Anyone who has driven our Land Rover up Fuzzball Lane and felt the wheels grip beneath the torrent and the gorse scourge its flanks will appreciate the outrageous machismo of the Land Rover marque; and that is why, whenever we saw this sissified urban cousin, we used to snicker.

That is why, when *GQ* handed me the keys to this 'Autobiography', with its satellite tracker and its leather seats as soft and pale as a poor little veal calf kept in a crate so that gross Italians may enjoy *vitello tonnato*, I felt, how shall I say, the beginnings of the old cynicism.

What is the point of all this size, you ask yourself, as you survey the world as though from the top of a camel or the howdah of an elephant? Why does the prow of this car need to stick out so arrogantly into the flow of traffic? What need is there for 58 cubic feet in the rear if all you are going to carry is a dog basket, green wellies and little Campaspe on her way to ballet classes?

I will even go so far as to say, without prejudicing my integrity, that this Range Rover is a magnificent machine.

Range Rovers never show the slightest sign of having scrabbled through the scree of Snowdonia, or roared out of some bog, or ploughed through the sea at low tide. You wouldn't dream of filling a Range Rover with logs, or lambs, or bales of hay – any of the useful things you can carry around a farm in its more macho cousin. This vehicle has a 4.6-litre engine and weighs 2,220 kilos, but in its soul it's a second-row forward dressed in a tutu. This was the gist of my complaint to my wife as we headed off for dinner one night. 'It's too showy,' I said, setting the autopilot for Cheyne Walk, where we were dining with a few nobs.

'Pure ostentation,' I declared. One of the extras you can have on the Autobiography is a TV and video. I suppose it might be useful on long journeys if the little brutes get tired of vomiting and beating each other up, but I wonder how well it fits in with the ethos of the marque. And as for this walnut burr finish – admittedly warm and lovely to the fingers but what's the point of it except to provide a convenient place for the wives of west African dictators to stick their chewing gum? 'Never,' I declared as we barged through traffic like a Chieftain tank, scattering the tourists like pigeons, 'has the spirit of Land Rover been so far removed from its roots.'

'Hey, what?' I snorted to my wife who, lulled by the floating gait of the vast machine, soothed by the soft zephyrs of the air conditioning and folded in the embrace of the leather chairs, seemed unaccountably to have lost the thread of what I was saying.

So I raved on until we reached our dinner and there, as the flashguns popped as I handed my wife down from the high step and we prepared to join Margaret Thatcher and assorted toffs, we experienced the adulation accorded those who own Range Rover Autobiographies. OK, I enjoyed it – the acclaim and the ride. It was like floating on a magic carpet. Never have I felt in such lordly command of the traffic. I will even go so far as to say, without prejudicing my integrity or kowtowing to the advertisers, that this Range Rover is a magnificent machine, probably worth every penny. But if you really want to arrive in style, in my view you should turn up in a 25-year-old Land Rover, with straw visibly adhering to your girlfriend's back.

Vital statistics

The Autobiography is designed to be the flagship for Range Rover's new bespoke car service.

Engine 2.5 to 4.6 litre, V8 petrol/diesel
Topspeed 122mph
Acceleration 0–60mph in 9.6 secs
Price (2000) £77,000

LEESON H

GERMANIC STREET

CREATURES

Porsche drivers weren't to Boris' taste until he floored the Boxster and developed a yen for the ultimate in flash.

Poor old Ferdinand Porsche. Back in Thirties Germany Ferdinand, you may recall, was Adolf's favourite car designer. He invented the Volkswagen Beetle, the people's car; that unassuming little scarab of a machine in which the *Volk* was to be transported in the fascist Elysium.

Little did he imagine, the great Ferdinand, what the word Porsche might, by the end of the century, mean to the modern British ear. Gone is the hint of democracy, that sense of a new technical advance dispersed throughout the families of the land. What the word Porsche once meant to the modern British ear – and I say this with the hesitation of one who has long wished to own an example of the marque – is 'wanker'.

Let us not beat about the bush. There were few hearts that did not sing for joy on that morning in October 1987, which financial historians refer to as 'Black Monday'. Many remember the stock market meltdown which happened that day, but for a few the memory is united with something more poetic, an image of cosmic justice – it was a Porsche 911 totalled by a falling tree. Crunched. Spiflicated. And, Thatcherite though we were as a nation, and, much as we approved, in principle, of the right of young men with teddy bears on their braces to make pots of money, we rejoiced to see their symbol smashed and made holiday in our hearts.

It grieves me to say this of such superb technology. And it obviously grieved the boys at Porsche, too. Which is why the heirs of Ferdinand decided to change the image. Hence the Boxster, which *is* a Porsche, but is not shaped like a mutant amphibian. Instead, the Boxster is shaped like a bar of soap, or one of those capsules full of vitamins which the French eat in large numbers or stick up their bottoms. In other words, you can't quite tell which is the bonnet and which is the boot.

The Boxster is shaped like a bar of soap, or one of those capsules full of vitamins which the French eat in large numbers or stick up their bottoms.

Yet as I infiltrated my body into the modestly sized cabin, the real question remained unanswered: in spite of all the efforts of Porsche's designers, is the car still synonymous with flash? In the sense that you can use your Porsche to travel much faster than you can in a Mercedes SLK or a Lotus Elise, the answer is most assuredly 'Yes.' It is also true that this Boxster has an absolutely beautiful convertible roof –

sinking back behind your head with nothing more than the murmur of a Bavarian bishop drumming his fingers on an ancient leather prie-dieu. Actually, the roof mechanism, with its dozens of motors, is so silent that I nearly decapitated my son, though perhaps we should not dwell on that point, lest it be seized on – either by my wife, or one of Tony Blair's tyrannical ministers as a further excuse for banning motor vehicles.

I also liked the speedometer with its understated dial, proceeding upwards in increments of 25mph. As I drove along the road, I occasionally let the animal out of the cage and we exploded forward in bursts like a stallion with wind. At the lights I became conscious of eyes on me from the left. I turned. It was a blonde, about 30, in a red Ford Escort. She gazed at me.

The roof mechanism is so silent that I nearly decapitated my son.

Was she thinking, 'Hello Big Boy, you Porsche-driving, groovy dude. Why don't you steer yourself in my direction?' Or was it more like: 'Get lost, flash git?' At that moment she roared away from the lights and I unaccountably stalled. It was only when we arrived at our common destination – my children's school – that the question was conclusively answered.

Maybe it is technically true that the Boxster's seats can accommodate two businessmen of fuller figure. All I can tell you is that to extricate one 35-year-old *GQ* motoring correspondent from the confines of that cabin, it would have been easier to start out with a block, tackle, pulley and lift. Finally I was free, wheezing on to the pavement, sprawled like a starfish under the appalled gaze of the mums. Did their eyes say 'flash git', as they beheld the vehicle? I think not. They loved the car, as did I, though as I struggled from all fours to regain my composure, it became clear; the *mot juste* was more like 'prat'. Flash prat. That was me.

Vital statistics

The Porsche Boxster S was launched into the two-seater sports market to compete with the Mercedes SLK and Lotus Elise 111S.

Engine 2.7-litre, 220bhp
Top speed 155mph
Acceleration 0–62mph in 6.6 secs
Price (2000) £42,161

DRIVING
BACK FROM
THE ABYSS

Boris tests the only Jaguar XKR-R in the country and decides he's not on the brink of a midlife crisis after all.

I have this awful dream. I'm playing football and I'm somewhere up near the opposition goal, when someone hits a long pass. Fantastic! It's rolling just there, not more than ten yards away from me, and there's not a defender in sight.

And so I make towards the ball and my brain says to my legs: 'Come on folks, sprint! Sprint like you used to, when there was spring in your heels, and the sap was rising.' And the boots clump forward, each one sucking slowly out of the mud. But there's something strange.

The legs are moving. But they won't move fast. My brain is shrieking: 'Run! Run! Damn you,' but the legs offer nothing but a lumpy skip and by now I'm starting to panic and I can feel my heart pounding, in terror not just of failure but of the evidence of mortality.

'Run, you bastards, run,' I moan. And there is no response, no acceleration, nothing but a stuttering waddle, and the defenders are arriving and the ball is trickling away and *aaaargh* …

Then I wake up. Or perhaps my wife hits me over the head with a pillow. At any rate, I sit there, bolt upright, sweating and pop-eyed and trying to pray. In that dark night, you stare into the black abyss of early middle age. You will never be fast again. You will never be as fast as you were.

No diet and no discipline will restore the electric snap and energy of youth. With the terrible candour that only comes at 3am, you know that your body is settling into a genetically programmed pattern of decay, and as you search for the consolations of advancing years, you know there are none. None at all.

There may be some, like me, who have been tempted in that moment to curse the Creator's cruelty in taking away our advantages one by one. To those people I say: whoa. Hang on. Before you top yourselves, let me tell you that the one fantastic advantage of getting older is that you might be able to afford the £60,105 (which is a fairly middle-aged kind of sum) to buy a Jaguar XKR-R. And that is why, when my heart is pattering pathetically in those dark nights of the soul, I let my mind wander back to just before Christmas, when I was at the wheel of this great greased cougar, this prowling panther prince of the road, capable of 155mph, with 370bhp and – *aaaaaah* – slowly the limbs unclench and I sink back on the pillow and I remember …

The Jaguar devoured the deserted A-road as though sucking the tarmac into its sabre-toothed maw.

We were late, and the M4 was chocker. Seventy miles away, a gang of kids was waiting for me to address them and, according to the clock-cum-navigation device tastefully inserted into the walnut fascia, we had only 26 minutes to get there. In theory, I was going to pick up Alex van Straubenzee, circulation manager of the

Spectator, at a Reading service station. He'd take the wheel, I'd write my speech, and we would roll up for dinner with the *Spectator* society of Marlborough school. In practice we now had 23 minutes to get there, and for all the use my beautiful, eight-cylinder engine (complete with four wonderful valves per cylinder) was, I might as well have been at the wheel of a Robin Reliant.

The gorgeous 18-year-old girls scrambled into the back of the Jaguar and ordered me to drive.

And now we had only 21 minutes to get there, and the pitiless satellite navigation device told me that I was still stuck behind the St Albans Sand & Gravel truck, just a spark, if viewed from the heavens, in the endless necklace of red tail-lights that was the M4. Then Alex came on the mobile, wondering where I was and we tried to stay cool, and smothered our guilt as we thought of those far-sighted Marlborough students who so admired our magazine as to found a society in its honour.

Then, thank Christ, we were at the service station. Alex was there. I threw on my black tie in the Little Chef car park, and we were off. Alex used to command troops in Ulster, and was obviously trained to evade terrorists at top speed. We howled down the motorway, Alex threading his way through the Volvos like Emerson Fittipaldi at a Monaco hairpin.

What an infamy, I thought as I scribbled my sermon, that the latest Bond film should not have chosen this fantastic British car, opting for one of those dawdling BMWs instead. And then, after a long stretch of deserted A-road, which the Jaguar devoured as though sucking the tarmac into its sabre-toothed maw, we were there. We were scrunching up the drive of this posh public school, somewhere near Swindon; in fact, we were only half an hour late.

And then came the best bit, the bit that sends me back to sleep with a smile. Marlborough is one of those public schools with a serious number of girls. After dinner, some of the society's leading lights said they wanted to see my motor. Indeed, when I told them it was the only Jaguar XKR-R coupé in the country, they seemed more interested in my car than my forthcoming speech.

And then – and for this I thank Jaguar, I thank whoever had a hand in making this epic machine – they scrambled into the back and ordered me to drive them. For a brief moment, I think that car made me vaguely interesting to these gorgeous 18-year-olds wearing low-cut ballgowns, with names like Georgina and Araminta. Not very interesting, just slightly more than I might otherwise have been. But isn't that enough?

Vital statistics

The XKR-R improves upon the standard XKR Coupé package by increasing brake and handling responses.

Engine 4-litre supercharged VS, 370bhp
Top speed 155mph
Acceleration 0–62mph in 5.2 secs
Price (2000) £66,005

MG À TROIS

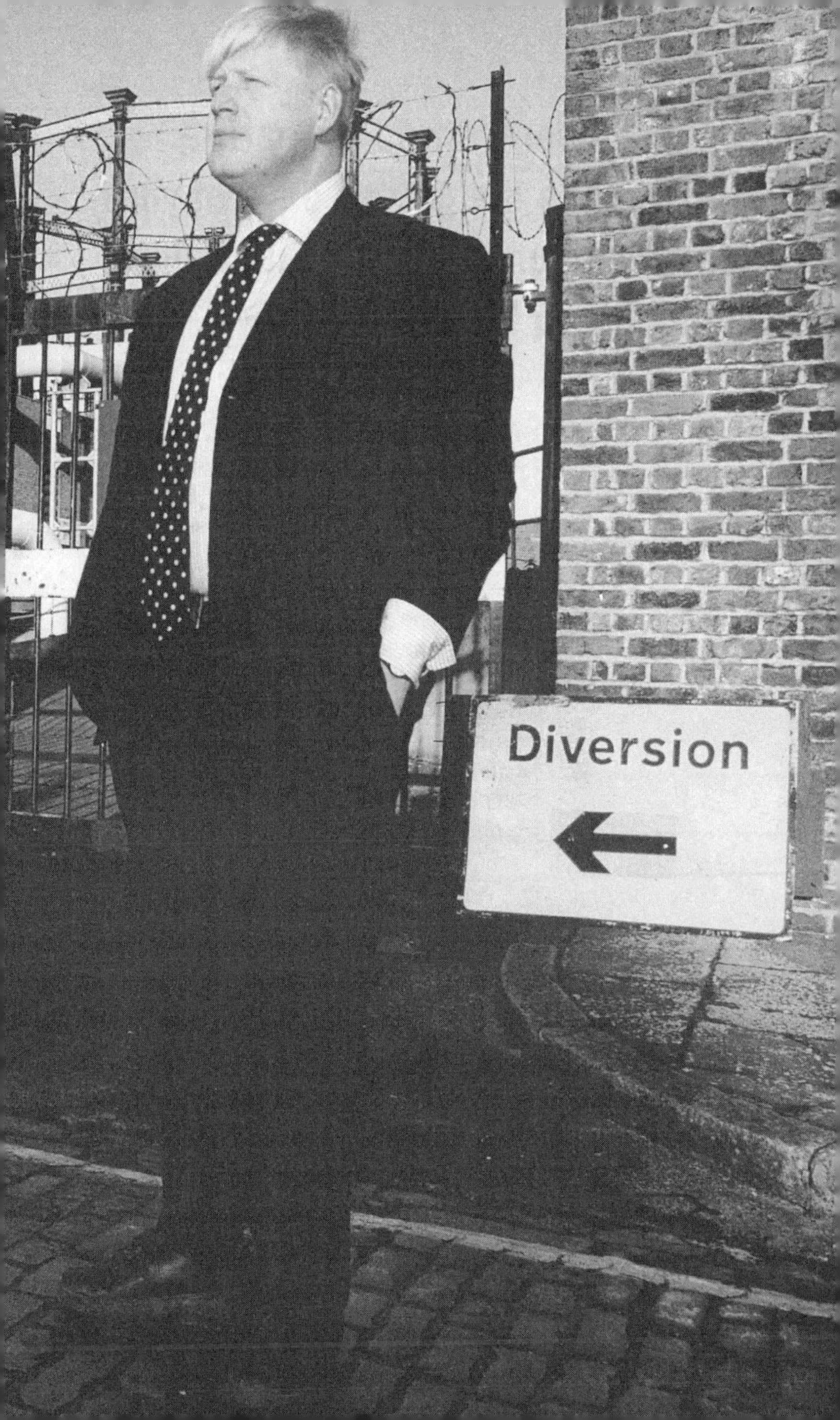
Diversion

Two's company, three's a party – Boris recalls the golden days of yore, riding shotgun in an MG with a fine young filly in his lap.

Ah yes, the octagonal bonnet boss, same as it ever was; the same procrustean effort to force yourself into the seat. The world has moved on in the 15 years since I last rode in an MG: life expectancy has increased by two years; the average weight of an airline passenger is four kilograms heavier; the female bust size has increased, on average, by a centimetre. But some things abide, some of the raw physical data of the universe will never change. And prime among them is that an MG has space only for two people, unless a third person is prepared to sit on someone's lap.

And with that thought my mind is transported back to 1984, those far-off, happy, balmy days when we were young, we were free, and we were just a bunch of poncey undergraduates. There was the girl; let us call her M. There was my pal; let us call him G. And there was the car, MG. I can hear it now, the roar of the balding wheels ping-ponging down the camber of the M40 in the days before they had it resurfaced. The girl's blonde hair is flying in the wind, mingling with the scent of Guerlain's Nahema. My friend G is driving with the utmost braggadocio, a lazy grin flitting across his face as we cut up the cars on the Headington roundabout; and the girl has decided not to sit on the gear stick but to perch on my lap – which was my secret plan.

Except that after a quarter of an hour of jouncing down the M40, the contours of my lap are, topographically speaking, beginning to resemble the gear stick. This is not good, I think. This is embarrassing, because the whole point of travelling in this vehicle is to impress her; to show suaveness and polish.

An MG is a long-nozzled, two-seater chickwagon, built for taking ladies for long, lazy picnics in Blenheim Park.

I want her to realise that I may not own a car like this myself, but I know a chap who does. And though this old MG, licence plate GAN668D, may be a clapped-out rust bucket; though pieces of aluminium ping off its hindquarters whenever my friend brakes sharply; though it has lost one of its headlights, the whole point is that it is an MG. A sports car, a long-nozzled, two-seater chickwagon: expressly built for taking ladies for long, lazy picnics in Blenheim Park; designed for joy and fun and seasons in the sun, and everything, in fact, except the mental torture of having the chick, with whom you are on friendly but by no means intimate terms, squirming on your lap in what can only be called a seriously frictional manner.

Oh boy oh boy, I mutter to myself. Stop it stop it, I groan as the sap rises and the ghastly hormones of youth begin to exercise their hydraulic spell. Has she noticed? And now we are overtaking another car, and my friend raises his black-gloved hand in an ironic salute to the driver (I think it may have been a Robin Reliant); and the girl turns to wave behind us, the sun glinting on her chic little pink sunglasses, and her chest is in my face and *ooooooof* ... Have you ever been in this sort of position?

What the hell does one do? You could always abandon efforts at self-control, and let her feel your feelings surging around. But how can you tell how a girl will react? Shock would be all right: a spot of gasping, nun-like shock. I could live with that. Simple embarrassment would be more or less OK. But what if she emits a peal of scornful laughter? Yes, it's the derision I worry about. I could handle anything except the derision.

And so I try all the psychological tricks I can, imposing the will on the flesh, just as Mahatma Gandhi used to invite nubile houris, clad in nothing but ankle bangles, to dance around him while he worked at his spinning wheel. *Ommmm*, I inwardly chant – sweat by now beading the brow – and try to picture myself weaving my lungi on packed earth somewhere in Delhi. No good. No good at all. Quick, try to think of something really deeply sad ... the death of a much-loved relative ... Ben Elton ... *ahhh!* That worked. But now we are passing the aerodrome, that flat stretch where we can see the early June countryside for miles around. The fields are bursting with crops; every tree is in maximum leaf, everything is green, every root and capillary engorged with the life-giving xylem and phloem, a livelier iris gleams on the burnished dove and *aaa*-tchoo! says the girl. She is prone to hay fever. And *kee-rist*, now she is sitting square on my lap, jiggling up and down. Will she notice? Worse still, will she fail to notice?

And then I am saved by the MG. We are on an incline and my friend G leans over and pulls a toggle. If memory does not deceive, it is labelled 'Supercharger'. G floors the throttle. We howl forward, brown smoke billowing from the rear, and we overtake another vehicle, a large vehicle full of admiring passengers. The girl stands up to take their salutes, and phew-eee, I am able to compose myself. Thank heavens for the MG. Thank goodness for the supercharger.

My friends, if you should be so lucky as to be a passenger in the MGF 1.8i Steptronic, with its accessory stainless-steel

Even with a gorgeous chick in your lap, all carnal feelings melt away before the charms of the MGF.

grille pack; and if you should find a gorgeous chick in your lap, then I can reassure you that such are the attractions of the car's gizmos – the stylish alloy gear knob, for instance; the signature fuel-filler cap, and the silver-faced dials – that you will be able to lose yourself in contemplation. Just as I was, eventually, lost in admiration of the supercharger.

Even the proximity of the girl and her soft, warm, stonewashed jeans, the smell of her hair: all will be sublimated, all carnal feelings melt away before the charms of the MG and, indeed, since my friend is now twiddling the wheel pretty freely, a fear of crashing. So go out and get one, or, better still, persuade a friend to buy one; get the girl, and if things are still in danger of becoming embarrassing, you can always ask to sit in her lap. These days, she'd probably suggest it immediately. That's another thing that has changed in the last 15 years.

Vital statistics

The new MGF's clutchless gearbox allows for manual acceleration with the ease of an automatic.

Engine 1.8i Steptronic, 120bhp
Top speed 118mph
Acceleration 0–60mph in 9.5 secs
Price (2000) £20,170

BRAND OF HOPE AND GLORY

Boris takes his son and heir for a spin in the AC Cobra V8, and discovers the automotive embodiment of his beloved Albion.

No trouble is too great for Dylan Jones, the saintly editor of *GQ* magazine. It was my son's fifth birthday and although I had taken a general role in approving the presents, none of them were directly attributable to me. There was the basketball hoop from the Early Learning Centre, given by his mother. There was the Pot Black mini-snooker game from his grandparents.

But where was the present from me to him, on this day, the first birthday that most children can remember? He was, of course, too polite to mention it, but the guilt welled up within. What a louse I was, spending all that time holed up in the office, churning out so many articles on European Monetary Union, smoking cigars and staring at the computer while – *choke!* – my little boy was – *sob!* – growing up without me and I was – *waaaah!* – too much of a selfish, sexist yuppie even to remember to get him a birthday present. But just as my eyes were misting at my blighted, misallocated life – *hark!*

The hush of Islington was broken by a low burble that turned into a roar and, as if in answer to my prayers, a shiny blue supercar parked outside the kitchen window. And I remembered: this was the day when Morgan, my point man at *GQ*, was bringing round the AC Cobra V8 – perhaps the butchest and most preposterously athletic car you've ever seen. I breathed a prayer of thanks to the gods of Condé Nast, and hailed my son.

'Son,' I said, or words to that effect, 'this is your birthday present. A ride in an AC Cobra V8 230bhp five-litre twin turbo.' And he was thrilled. Or at least I jolly well hope he was. He blooming well should have been. Because this car is a piece of living motoring history. All the other great British sporting marques have died or been bought. Did you play Top Trumps when you were a nipper? You remember the unbeatable ones?

There was the Jensen Interceptor III, the Aston Martin and the Jaguar E-type. Now the old Jensen is on the scrapheap, and the others have been taken over by Americans. Only AC lives on as an independent British concern. AC is, as the promo blurb says, 'the quintessentially British sports car, hand-built by British craftsmen', and from the moment we buckled ourselves into that cockpit, surrounded by blue carbon fibre – as blue as the empyrean sky on a summer's eve in 1940, when the Spitfires had just sent the last

German fighters packing – we knew that this was going to be a truly British experience.

'Isn't this fantastic?' I said to the heir to the Johnson millions, as we sat in the open-top cabin. His reply was hard to make out, since he had for some reason decided to wear a tiger mask, perhaps in the hope of not being recognised. Just to sit on the black leather of that driver's seat – talk about British! It was as snug as the 5.25 Connex South Central from Victoria to Horsham on a Friday, or Geri Halliwell's Union Jack thong.

The engine was like an old English organ revving up for the final chords of 'Jerusalem'.

When I turned on the ignition, the music of the engine was like the organ of some old English school, revving up for the final crashing chords of 'Jerusalem' on the last day of term, while all the school leavers start to blub; and the smoke of the exhaust hung in the air like the breath of a hot Cornish pasty on a cold Cornish beach. I crunched the car into first: I mean really crunched, like Wade Dooley's outstretched fist connecting with the nasal bones of the French number eight.

And *varooom*, we were off, and I think, so far as I could tell given the tiger mask, the kid was excited. Oh, you will tell me that the engine isn't really British, since it's made by Ford; and I will say to you, so what? Look at the Trident sub, Britain's independent nuclear deterrent. It is two-thirds US-built, yet it is Trident: modified and controlled by us British, just as Britannia waves her three-pronged fork in mastery of the azure main. That is the sense in which the AC Cobra is British.

Who cares about the exact provenance of the engine, when the fuselage is as light and delicious and distinctively British as one of Mrs Beeton's macaroons? We thrummed out on to Liverpool Road, turned left at Holloway Road, and then we were at the nearest thing my neck of the woods has to a grand prix track – the first stretch of Camden Road up to the lights.

Sir Malcolm Campbell in his Bluebird might have beaten us up the hill. But I doubt it.

As I was about to open the throttle, I turned to my son, just as Cockroft must have turned to Walton just before they split the atom; or as Armstrong must have turned to Buzz Aldrin the moment before opening the hatch of the lunar module. Whatever happened, things would never be the same again. 'OK, son?' I said, or words to that effect, and pressed my foot to the floor.

Unfortunately the car came to a sudden halt, since the brake, clutch and accelerator

are all confusingly close to one another –
as British in their mutual proximity as the
stumps of a wicket. But never mind; it was
the work of a moment to turn the motor
again and let her have it. Maybe, if Sir
Malcolm Campbell had been next to us in
his Bluebird and had been determined to
break the land speed record, maybe he
would have beaten us up the hill. But I
doubt it. I can see why the makers of the
AC Cobra didn't bother with a roof. There's
probably some law of physics showing that
raindrops are incapable of penetrating the
slipstream and hitting the occupants. It was
pure joy. It was a few seconds of bliss. And
the reaction of the crowd, as we made our
triumphal return down Holloway Road? It
was truly British.

In America they would have shouted
'Way to go!' Here, with supreme effort, they
ignored us. One man did shout 'prick!' but
he was driving an old orange Escort, so I
think we can take that as a compliment.
As for the five-year-old, he was almost
overcome by the whole thing. As he put it
himself, 'Can we go home now?'

Vital statistics

The new AC
Superblowers use
carbon fibre to create a
much lighter frame
which allows for greater
acceleration.

Engine 5-litre, V8,
230bhp
Top speed 145mph
Acceleration 0–60mph
in 5.2 secs
Price (2000) £38,950

EXTRA STRONG TINTS

After a string of motoring mishaps that really weren't his fault, Boris encases himself in blacked-out glass and chauffeur-driven luxury.

The man came closer. His face was almost next to mine. I could see the pores in his horrible nose. His eyes had an unfocused, moronic look, and a trickle of drool ran from the corner of his mouth. With cool deliberation, I raised my hand and thumbed my nose at him, right there in his face.

He didn't move. I blew a raspberry. For a while he remained rooted. He licked his lips and, like a man who knows he is beaten, withdrew. But haven't we all felt like him sometimes?

Suppose you're tootling around on your bike and one of those massive white cars comes past. It's so big that it pushes you into the kerb and, as you curse and try not to fall off, you find yourself staring into the tinted windows. What's going on in there? Why this ostentatious modesty?

I don't know about you, but my assumption has always been that these cars are ferrying some sort of nightclub entrepreneur to the East End. What the tinted windows are saying is: 'Oi, you can't look into my car 'cos I am snorting cocaine while my extremities are being refreshed by Mindy and Cindy and Mandy and Candy ...'

That's the point of the tinted window, isn't it? It is a taunt to the rest of the law-abiding public, who, like poor Gillian Taylforth, know that standard-issue windows offer no protection from nosiness. At least, that's what I thought until I spent a day with the Men In Black.

For some reason, *GQ* seems increasingly reluctant to let me drive. I am lucky, nowadays, if I'm allowed more than a day with a car. OK, so I am sorry about that bit that fell off the Jag; and it wasn't my fault that the Jap supercar was removed from the *Spectator* offices by crane. The ding on the Porsche was unfortunate, and the parking tickets were just an occupational hazard. But, for whatever reason, the motoring editor decided that rather than chew his nails, he would have me chauffeured about for a day.

My driver came at the crack of dawn and had with him one of those Chrysler Voyager people-wagons. It is a great tribute to the confidence Men In Black has in its drivers' abilities, as these brash Yank vans did famously badly in the European NCAP crash tests.

I pointed this out to my driver. He took it well. We drove to my office. On the way, I practised sprawling on the black leather banquette and found it easy, but somehow unsatisfactory. What is the point of sprawling on your own? What about the female cup-bearers and the Moët? There was a rack of champagne glasses, but no bottle. According to my driver the last occupants had been Mike Tyson's bodyguards and trainer and they are abstemious Muslims.

What is the point of sprawling on your own? What about the female cup-bearers and the bottles of Moët?

So there I was, mooching on the non-bonking banquette, twiddling my empty champagne glass and wondering when the sense of hedonistic rapture would begin, when I looked out of the window.

There, leering at me, was the man with the spongiform nose. Heaven knows what he thought was going on inside – Naomi Campbell being pleasured by Dorking Rugby Club's second XV, or something equally decadent.

In fact, there was nothing but me reading the paper. That's probably the real reason stars have tinted windows. They don't want the world to know the dismal truth: that they are just sitting there picking their noses. In fact, when one considers the ordeal of watching one's fellow motorists at traffic lights, all of them a-probing and a-delving, one can see the case for making tinted windows mandatory.

Vital statistics

Men In Black has both male and female chauffeurs and is a favourite with pop stars and celebs. Complimentary champagne, soft drinks and a choice of DVD and video games are all part of the service.

Price (2000) £340 per day; £50 per hour

SUSHI
QUATTRO

Japanese car, Italian name,
Brit-designed body – the Delfino's
mixture set Boris thinking …

It has been a wrench to say goodbye to Morgan, the *GQ* car impresario who used to turn up on my doorstep every month with the latest throbbing apparatus, but who has now sought pastures new. Perhaps he was already losing his focus when he came with his final offering because, frankly, he didn't have a clue what it was.

'Ere,' I said, when the engine had died down, and it stood there, vast, black, glossy and enigmatic, like Frank Bruno after one punch too many. 'Ere,' I said, 'so what do you call this, then?' Morgan consulted the bonnet boss. 'It says Delfino,' he announced confidently.

There was a time when the construction of a new car in Britain was a matter of national pride and the deepest political engagement. I remember the excitement when John DeLorean came to Northern Ireland and offered to construct a gull-winged car; and I remember the huge cash dowry he was given by the people of this country; and when, of course, it turned out that DeLorean was a bit of a con man, I remember the grief and shame of the nation.

And now look at us. See what 20 years of Thatcherism has taught us. See the ruthlessness and variety of the market. If the Delfino story is anything to go by, there are new cars being invented every day in this country, and no one seems to notice, and you certainly don't find the taxpayer being called upon to subsidise them.

It turns out that the Delfino is the brainchild of one Allard Marx who, unlike the Detroit-trained DeLorean, knows absolutely nothing about cars. He is a marketing man.

A few years ago he was paid by a dodgy company to come up with a name for a sports car. He chose Delfino (Italian for 'dolphin'), only to watch the company go down the pan. So he took the name to a couple of engineers who were developing a more realistic sports car project – Andrew Borrowman and Sean Prendergast.

If Arnold Schwarzenegger looks like a condom stuffed with walnuts, then the Delfino is like a bin liner containing a couple of televisions.

The trio fished around for a suitable foundation for their new machine, finally settling on the Subaru Impreza Turbo – a sort of Jap supercar which is currently demolishing the competition on the world's rally circuits at the hands of Britain's very own Richard Burns. They added a big-bore exhaust and a K&N air filter, and swaddled the shiny metal bits in GRP monocoque shell. That is why it goes so fast: the car is a third lighter than a normal Impreza Turbo, which is itself pretty damn quick, hitting 60mph in just 6.5 seconds.

Our normal test route to the offices of the *Spectator* confirmed that the Delfino does indeed go like the clappers. It is a big, butch, two-seater sports car, with those exaggerated fibreglass bulges about the fore and hindquarters which are meant to be suggestive of the muscular ridges you see on bodybuilders. If Arnold Schwarzenegger looks like a condom stuffed with walnuts, then the Delfino is like a bin liner containing a couple of televisions.

On reaching our destination Morgan and I got out and gazed at the alloy wheels, the great grey baleen of the radiator grille, and were none the wiser. What the hell was it? Why had it been put on earth, this anthracite Batmobile? What was its ethic? Its charter? What was the point of it?

Why had it been put on earth, this anthracite Batmobile? What was its ethic, its charter?

But the truly sensational thing about the Delfino is that it does not in any meaningful sense exist. There is no Delfino factory as yet, and there won't be until Allard Marx has found a suitable location and enough people prepared to pay £67,600 to invest in the company, which entitles you to one Delfino and a one per cent share in the equity! Amazing!

As my brain struggles to grasp the brilliance of Mr Marx's business plan, I see a new future for us all. In the great global free market of today, we can all be car pioneers; we can all be Allard Marx. As I look out of the window at my wife's ancient Peugeot 409 (left-hand drive but with a pretty aggressive 1.6 engine provided you give it lots of choke) the idea grows in my mind.

Just get some new alloy wheels, swathe the thing in black GRP monocoque and *voilà*: meet the new Johnson Caramba or Anaconda or Siesta. All I need is a big PR launch. Forget about the dotcoms. Forget the 'new economy'. Let's all make cars! Never has it been so easy to do a start-up.

Vital statistics

The team behind the Delfino chose to use the Subaru Impreza's underpinnings because its cult status and bulletproof reliability would encourage potential customers to take the car seriously.

Price (2000) £39,500

I CAME, I SAW, I PLAYED WITH THE GADGETS

Faced with the decadent, sophisticated splendour of Mercedes' S55 AMG, Boris can't help feeling a bit of a barbarian.

I'm sorry, Hans and all the guys at Stuttgart. Please don't think me ungrateful. But a lot of this stuff is just wasted on me. I know the Mercedes S55 AMG is the most technically advanced model yet produced by your great company. I had a lovely weekend threading through the lanes of Sussex, cornering like a sinuous torrent of molten metal.

I have nothing but praise for the interior, the engine, everything. It is just that I felt somehow inadequate as I looked at the range and complexity of your refinements; I simply felt unable to offer any opinion.

It was like being a Visigoth turning up in Rome and then being invited to take supper with a senator from one of the older families. Your host offers you peacock stuffed with dormice, followed by larks'-tongue patties, and then asks you what you think of his statue of Apollo, and have you read Catullus? What are you supposed to say? The whole thing is beyond you. You have never seen such sophistication.

Such were my feelings as I sat in the cabin and enjoyed the benefits of the automatic climate-control system. Do you know what they've come up with, these boffins? They have sensors which can detect the position of the sun and, if the sensors work out that the sun is shining on your seat, special air-conditioning nozzles are turned up to compensate, adjusting the microclimate in your vicinity. Sensational. And if you sway in your seat as the car takes a corner, the belt is tightened round your midriff.

Talking of seats, you don't just sit down in this Merc. You can twizzle your seat up, down, forwards and back, as though working your way through a sex manual with an uncomplaining and untiring partner. There is the dentist's chair, the scrunched-up Lilo effect, the buttock-clencher for fast driving, and the fully extended bonk position. Secreted somewhere in the back rest is a computer-controlled masseur.

Please don't think me ungrateful. But a lot of this stuff is just wasted on me.

Yes, you get in-seat massage. Mercedes has created a pulsating chamber of air that relaxes the discs and muscles of the back. As soon as you click in your seat belt, the rear head restraints emerge and cup your skull, like the soft hands of a geisha. If your thighs are too warm on the leather, a special thermostat is used to cool them down; and if they are too cold, then the boys from Mercedes have come up with a way of heating them up, rather as you used to get your fag to warm up the bog-seats on those bitter winter mornings at school.

On the steering wheel are buttons that enable you to phone the wife, watch television, buy stocks and shares and launch a hostile bid for a FTSE-100 company, without taking your hands off the wheel. The sunroof has a memory, so that it will roll back to the position in which it was last used. The steering wheel raises its head as you slide your legs beneath it and then bows again, submitting to your controlling hands. So obedient is this car

You don't just sit down in this Merc. You can twizzle your seat up, down, forwards and back, as though working your way through a sex manual with an uncomplaining and untiring partner.

that it doesn't even require that you open it with a key. No: special radars detect whether or not you are carrying the key in your pocket and, if you are, the car will recognise you, just as Argus, the old blind dog of Odysseus, recognised his master after a gap of 20 years. Just reach for the handle, and the car will admit you with the silent aplomb of a butler.

My friends, this is luxury: all I ask is are we worth it? Do we deserve it, this mollycoddling? I think of my grandfather, a man who fought in the war. He had a Merc, which he bought in Egypt in the Thirties. For many years it sat in the farmyard, grass shooting through its fender, the geese laying eggs on the back seat.

But my family always knew that it was a special car, a distinguished car. For us, it was always The Mercedes, a symbol of bygone ease and grace. And what was its most luxurious feature? Perhaps it was the wing mirror, which automatically told you whether or not you needed a shave. Perhaps it was the seats, which had special bouncy things in them called springs.

I don't know. All I know is that our concept of luxury has changed out of all recognition. Look at us all: soft, indolent, foul-mouthed, pampered and caressed whenever we get in a car. What would my grandfather make of it all? Was this why his generation fought and died – so we could be given electronic massage in our Mercs?

What would his reaction have been to the wanton extravagance of the S-class? Might he not have scorned us? Might he not have dismissed it as a car for sissies? Actually, I think he might have been rather interested. Particularly in the seats.

Vital statistics

Until 1999 AMG was an independent firm that specialised in tuning Mercedes. But it did such a good job that Merc bought 51 per cent of its shares.

Engine 5.5-litre V8, 360bhp
Top speed 156mph
Acceleration 0–62mph in 6 secs
Price (2000) £84,000

THRUSTING FOR THE HUSTINGS

Boris puts the MP into Impreza as he heads for his moment of political destiny in the terrifically turbocharged Subaru.

Think of the great historic rides. Think of Paul Revere, galloping from Lexington to Concord to warn the American militias that the English were coming. What did he say to his steed? Did he flog its foaming flanks? Did he yell encouragement? Or, like me, as I charged from London to Thame, did he do both?

'Come on there, boy!' I yipped to my mount, as I belaboured its leather steering wheel. 'Come on,' I whispered into its air-conditioning ducts, 'you can do it, you little beauty, you jouncy Japanese jackrabbit. Just get me there by 11am and I'll give you the juiciest write-up *GQ* has ever seen.' And why was I in such a tearing hurry that I whispered to a mere machine, even if it was as sophisticated as the

Subaru Impreza Turbo 2000 AWD saloon?

It was because democracy stood at the crossroads. My career had reached a turning-point and if I was late by so much as a minute, it would fail to turn. More than 30 miles up the M40 they were waiting for me, the most exacting audience a man can face. It was the Henley Conservative Association, and I was applying to be their prospective parliamentary candidate. And let me tell you something, all the many of you who are, I hope, thinking of doing the same in other constituencies.

If your shoes are not polished to the reflectiveness of mirrors, they will not mind; if your haircut is a bit eccentric, they will not hold it against you. But if you keep them waiting for as much as 30 seconds, you are sunker than the *Graf Spee*. I had only 45 minutes before I was due to attend their pleasure and the motorway was rigid with Saturday morning traffic.

What could I do? What could I say to the car, all its kinetic energy held in potential? The sun beat down on the rows of boiling bonnets and I could feel the machine sucking the air greedily into the aggressive-looking intake. And in spite of the efficiency of the air conditioning, I grew hotter and hotter. Did any of the great horses of history have to queue like this, as they carried their masters towards some decisive contest? Did Bucephalus have to dawdle, his nose pressed to the rump of a second-rate donkey or packhorse as he conveyed Alexander to the battle of the Issus in 333 BC?

Did Napoleon sit chewing the reins of his horse, Marengo, hopelessly bogged down in the traffic there on the Brussels road on June 17, 1815? Did Wellington, coming in the opposite direction, find that his beloved nag, Copenhagen, was surrounded by slower beasts, and unable to take him faster than the slowest gun carriage? Of course not! That is why the great generals of the past were equipped with these fabulous beasts, so that when history accelerated, they could accelerate too.

That is why, for a moment or two, when the traffic finally eased up and the gap between the cars opened up first to an axe-handle's length, and then a cricket pitch, I thought of behaving badly. For a second or so, it occurred to me that I could exploit the privilege of driving this Subaru; perhaps I should behave with all the arrogance of a member of the Labour politburo. As it happens, I have since been to Moscow, where I found people absolutely riveted by the affair of 'Zhak Strov', as Jack Straw is called on the Russian radio, and his ton-up driver.

The Impreza is so tuned, so terrific, that as soon as a gap appears, you're through.

'I cannot believe this,' said my friend Dmitri, 'what is his job, this Zhak Strov? He is your interior minister, no?' Dmitri and the rest of the Russian public are greatly tickled that Mr Strov should have been stopped for allowing himself to be driven at 103mph. Incredible, said Dmitri, pointing at a tint-windowed Mercedes going like the clappers, surrounded by motorcycle outriders: in Russia, if a traffic cop were to be so foolish as to stop a member of the regime for speeding, he'd find himself redeployed in Irkutsk. To the Russian mind, it is self-evident that there is one traffic law for the elite, and one for everyone else; and indeed, to judge by his behaviour, and the fact that no one is being prosecuted for an offence that normally results in you losing your licence, that is the principle upon which Mr Straw himself is operating.

And yes, to be frank, my own mind was moving in that direction. Surely, I reasoned, as the hour of my appointment drew closer, these are extenuating circumstances? Surely a policeman would understand my special need? But no, said my conscience; come, come, it said. And so I didn't do a Jack Straw; and I didn't use excessive speed: well, I certainly didn't do anything which could warrant losing a licence.

So tuned, so terrific was the Subaru, that I had no need. By the sheer friskiness of its acceleration, I was able to weave the car through the traffic. When you're driving an Impreza, as soon as a gap appears you can just squeeze down gently with your big toe, the rev counter whirls round, and you're through.

With five minutes to go, I tottered through the doors of the motel. I will not pretend that it was a triumph of oratory. But it was more or less OK. If there was one question which went well, it was this. 'Mr Johnson,' they said, 'you seem to be a busy man. How are you going to manage to travel from London to this constituency, and fulfil all your commitments?'

'Mr Chairman,' I said, 'it so happens that the answer is standing in the car park outside.'

Vital statistics

British rally driver Richard Burns was odds-on favourite to win the World Rally Championship in his Impreza WRC.

Engine 2-litre, 16V 4-cylinder, 218bhp
Performance 143mph, 0–62mph in 8.2 secs
Price (2000) £26,390

ROOFLESS
CAPITALISM

Boris baits his pinko neighbours with the proudly plutocratic Rolls-Royce Corniche.

Just look at that. *Slookathat*, I said to myself, after I had finished parking. All you need do was squint. You just cropped the image in your head.

Here was my street in darkest London N7, where the badlands of Holloway began, and the pavements were barricaded with big yellow police notices begging for help with the latest stabbing. Sometimes the drug dealers were parked two deep outside the pub. But today all you had to do was blank them out, forget about the council housing and the litter, and just imagine you were an estate agent taking a still for use in the window. Just get the chestnut, with the conkers starting to swell. Get the house – the one opposite mine, as it happens: a sizable, white-stuccoed semi; and then get the car in the foreground. Filter out the rest. Yes, just let the car do the talking and what a message it sent.

There he stood – the whingeing Rolls disser, the hater of duty, the leveller.

Sodding millionairesville, said the car. It looked like the Johnson family, after generations of toil in the beeswax factories of Erzurum, and as itinerant fairground wrestlers, had arrived. *Slookathaaat*, I breathed again, as I looked at £250,000 worth of motor car, with its eight cylinders comprising a cubic capacity capable of getting through more fuel in half an hour than William Hague can put away in a day delivering soft drinks. No, I said to myself, as I gazed at the Rolls-Royce Corniche, there can be no one alive who looks on this piece of engineering and feels anything but pride in human attainment.

Is there anyone so mean as to resent the Spirit of Ecstasy and all she stands for? I twanged the Winged Victory affectionately, testing her curious springy moorings on the prow of the car, rather as one might twang a tentative bra strap. Was anybody still so prissy as to call this car vulgar? Could a man look upon the shag-pile blue carpet, the great cerulean sweep of steel above the rear wheel, curling and spreading like some rolling wave at Polzeath, and not be turned into a sap, a soft-head, a complete Corniche patsy? Was there any of us who would not be affected by the beauty of the burred walnut fascia, the white leather seats as soft as the purse of some Saudi *poule de luxe*?

I think I may have emitted a low moan, a carnal whimper; and at that moment, just as I was looking around for someone to share my joy, I heard a voice. 'Oi!' said a chippy snarl. 'How long are you going to park that thing there?'

'Hey?' I whipped round and – wait: who do you think it was? Whose soul was so stewed in bile that he had taken against my Rolls? No, my friend, it was not some socially inadequate parking warden. It wasn't some typical character from the Holloway Road, the man who sits on the bench with a can of Special Brew; it wasn't some taut-nerved single mum making her

Vital statistics

According to Rolls, most Corniche buyers will have at least six other cars cluttering up their garage.

Engine 6.75-litre, 16V, 8-cylinder, 325bhp
Performance 135mph, 0–60mph in 8 secs
Price (2000) £250,000

way to the cash converters in the hope of pawning her baby's buggy. I'll tell you who it was, the whingeing Rolls-disser, the hater of duty, the leveller. There is only one type of person, these days, who can fail to be moved as he gazes into the 16 shimmering coats of paint, minutely applied with toothbrushes by the craftsmen of Crewe; and that is an Old Etonian member of the Labour Party, who sees his own reflection in the Roller's burnished flank and feels the rage of Caliban.

Standing behind me was a member of Islington's haute bourgeoisie, the editor of a left-wing magazine. I will not embarrass him by telling you his name. Suffice it to say that he supports higher taxation, especially of motorists.

I scanned his face for signs of irony. Surely he was kidding. But no. His usually amiable features were a mask of embarrassment. 'Do you think you might get around to moving it?' he asked, through bared teeth. And we both understood.

My friend has spent half a lifetime in the toils of middle-class guilt. When someone uses his house as the backdrop for a Rolls-Royce Corniche, a car worth about as much as a small Loire chateau or a terraced street in Scunthorpe, he feels no joy, none of the simple things that you or I would feel. He feels only terror that someone – someone he knows – might think the car belonged to him; and that his cred as a member of the left-leaning Blairite liberal intelligentsia would be destroyed. And so I moved it, because it pained me to see him that way; and everywhere we went the car worked its magic on the landscape. We parked at the tennis courts, and at once the players of Highbury Fields, with their knock knees and black socks and dribbling serves, seemed to take on the sheen of money and style. We went up towards Seven Sisters Road, and the ill-favoured stall-holders instantly had something of the Burlington Arcade.

Down Farringdon Road we went, past the *Guardian* office, national epicentre of the politics of resentment, and look – was that Hugo Young leaning out of his office, cheering? Was that Polly Toynbee in a leotard, high-kicking down the pavement as we passed? I'm not sure. All I can say is that as we passed a notoriously right-on pub, people raised their beer and toasted us with loud acclaim. Yes, my experience with the ultimate Roller taught me this: that 20 years of Thatcherism and post-Thatcherism have utterly changed attitudes in this country to money and towards conspicuous consumption. These days, to drive a Corniche is not to be a top-hatted slimeball who grinds the faces of the poor. It is to show nothing but an innocent financial exuberance, a touching pleasure in ostentation. And when I returned and parked again outside my chum's house – there being no other space – I watched him closely. I wish you could have been there to see his liberal sneer contort and dissolve into a grin, an irrepressible beam of appreciation.

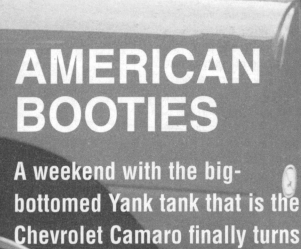

AMERICAN BOOTIES

A weekend with the big-bottomed Yank tank that is the Chevrolet Camaro finally turns Boris into a Euro-enthusiast.

Under almost any circumstances I am a fervent pro-American. You say Big Mac is a culinary disaster. I say yum-scrum. You say Disney is an abomination, destroying old European fairy stories, rotting our children's minds. I say, I love you, Pocahontas, baby, and you too, Lion King.

Come on over here and rape our culture, you cute little Mickey Mouse, go right ahead, be my guest. I share the American dream, the get-up-and-go, Route 66, drive-by shootings, Have A Nice Day. You can keep your English breakfast. Give me a pile of hamburgers with bacon and maple syrup followed by a flash-fried frazzfurter, washed down with lashings of root beer. I even quite like the look of Britney Spears.

Yup, maybe it's because one of my great-grandparents was American, but there are scarcely any questions of taste or politics on which I will not defend America. Until, that is, you put me in front of a creation from Detroit. When suddenly I become a pro-European of the most violent, dyspeptic and incurable disposition.

I'm Jacques Delors, Ken Clarke and Michael Heseltine rolled into one. On the issue of which continent makes the best cars, the home of Ferrari or the home of Chevrolet, I am a raving Euro-federalist. Nothing you say will convince me that Americans have a clue how to make a decent sports car, and certainly not the great trundlewagon called the Chevrolet Camaro.

America has been called the Land of the Free. A better name would be the Land of the Fat. You get in this car and even if, like

CHEVROLET CAMARO

me, you weigh almost 16 stone, you have this sense that the driver's seat was built to cradle arses vaster than our society can yet comprehend. This isn't a sports car; it's a glorified chaise longue for the kind of mega-buttocked American security guard who spends all day dunking donuts until that special second belly appears under the belt and he has to be cantilevered into his Chevy with a block and tackle. OK, it's comfy. But where is the paciness, the urgency, the slightly hysterical prestissimo styling of an Alfa?

This isn't a sports car: it's a glorified chaise longue for mega-buttocked Yanks.

Ahead of you stretch yards of pseudo-aerodynamic red metal, a great pretence of a sporting bonnet; but when you turn the key, what do you get? You get a murmur about as thrilling as the hum of air-conditioning in a Howard Johnson motel. So you slam your foot down, because it seems inconceivable that a car so streamlined should not have a trick up its sleeve. And what happens?

The fuel gauge flickers and you get a sort of lollop, and then the lollop breaks into a potter, and then into a trundle, until finally you achieve the kind of speeds you would have achieved ten seconds ago in a European machine.

Camaro? you think to yourself. What the hell is a camaro anyway? As you limp homewards, overhauled by Motability rickshaws, you debate which animal the boys at Chevrolet had in mind. A stallion, perhaps, a wild horse of the Camargue? No: the suffix is all wrong. You get home. You look it up. You can't believe it.

Camaro is Spanish for a kind of shrimp, which just about sums it up.

Camaro is Spanish for a kind of shrimp, which just about sums it up: a gleaming red carapace, and nothing very frightening within.

I don't blame Chevrolet. I blame Jimmy Carter. The Americans have such cheap gasoline that they can run these vast cars. But federal US law says they cannot exceed 55mph. That's why the poor old Camaro toddles along like a sheep dressed as a greyhound. There's no point in being able to accelerate from 0–60mph in six seconds if you are breaking the law after you hit 55mph.

It's not as if the car is altogether ridiculous. The roof is terrific, and somehow so designed that you stay warm even when you have it down on a cold day, as though the windshield creates an air pocket. If only, I thought sadly, if only those American manufacturers had the incentive to build engines as we do in Europe.

And then it hit me: the solution.

Vital statistics

A 5.7-litre, 158mph version of the Camaro, the Z28, is available for £22,500 from selected Vauxhall dealers.

Engine 3.6-litre V6, 190bhp
Performance 125mph, 0–60mph in 8.5 secs
Price (2001) £21,505

Don't tell me that the US emits less CO_2 as a result of Carter's speed limit. Most American greenhouse gases are produced by flatulent cattle and hamburgers. What America needs is somebody to persuade her to raise the speed limit to European levels, and I have the answer.

If I have a mission in life, it is to end the senseless division of the west into rival European and American trade blocs. Then the Americans may understand the joy of our speed limits, just as we appreciate Mickey Mouse. And perhaps, one day, as both sides benefit from mutually civilising influences, they will build better sports cars as a result.

REMEMBRANCE
OF THINGS
FAST

Boris recalls how he found poetic power beneath the hood of the Maserati 3200 GT.

You know how it is, when you dissect a rat in some teenage biology lesson and you're suddenly filled with the wonder of nature. No, make that a nobler animal: a deer, perhaps.

We were walking once along the bank of the river when some hounds brought the stag to bay before our eyes and, in less than a minute, the beast had been shot and gralloched on the grass. *Zip* went the knife, and it all came spilling out: the organs, the tubes, all as carefully packed as a silken parachute. If you have ever seen such a thing – the bluish organs with their white cauls of fat, the long pulsing pipes, everything folded and fitted according to some mysterious pattern – then like me you've probably thought, 'Crumbs. I wonder whether it is really possible that all this was put together by accident?'

Surely, you think, there was a maker at work here. Only a mind, a planner, a genius could have come up with this amazing system for turning grass and turnips into the speed and grace of a deer. Were you of a spiritual disposition, you might sink to your knees by the steaming corpse there and then and, opening your hymn book at number 354, 'All Things Bright and Beautiful', give warbling thanks to the heavenly Creator.

Well, such were my feelings, more or less, on getting home after a long drive and opening the bonnet of the Maserati 3200 GT. I gazed in ignorance, an ignorance surpassing even that of my knowledge of biology. Look how much has been crammed in: the great big fat long things, the vast doodah with the squiggly bits coming out of the, er. Just look at those sucking, flaring thingumajigs leading straight into the whatnot. And there in the middle, a gigantic piece of drop-forged metal, silver and glistening, and still pinking gently after its exertions.

I gazed and wondered why it might be arranged in eight bar-shaped convexities, like the abdomen of a body-builder. Was it the cylinder head, and did the eight bars somehow correspond to the eight cylinders? Or was it the big end? The jobby? Who knows? And there, Christ on a bike, look at those arterial red valve affairs – the ventricles, the aortas, the something-or-others. All I can safely report is that there is a magic in the innards of this animal.

All I can safely report is that there is a magic in the innards of this animal.

The boffins at Maserati have taken a century-old idea that you can burn petrol, and they have turned it – yes, call me pretentious, I don't give a stuff – into magic and poetry. Millions of years ago, forests perished in the Persian Gulf. It wasn't a very interesting business to watch, one imagines, just leaves falling from trees, settling on decomposing dinosaurs, creating a treacly black soup. But look what this car can do if you give it some of that old soup. There has never been a machine which so perfectly alchemised fuel into beauty, poise, grace, speed.

There has never been a machine which so perfectly alchemised fuel into beauty, poise, grace, speed.

Vital statistics

The Maserati 3200 GT uses the latest 'drive-by-wire' technology and has electronically adjustable suspension.

Engine 3.2-litre V8, 370bhp
Performance 174mph, 0–62mph in 5.1 secs
Price (2001) £60,950

I can't tell you exactly why I loved driving this car so much. I flipped through the brochure in search of some adjectives and found the advertising copywriters reduced to babble. It says the pleasure of driving a Maserati is all about 'the emotion of discovering sensations that have always been exclusive: characteristics with a timeless appeal by searching for the new'. It sounds a lot better in Italian, so here it is. The pleasure of driving a Maserati is, '*l'emozione di riconoscere caraterri da sempre privilegiati segni che restano nel tempo attraverso la ricerca del nuovo.*' I don't know about you, but I have a feeling that this is bullshit in any language.

I tell you what it's about. It's the light in the eyes of our 24-year-old blonde receptionist when she heard that I had a Maserati parked outside, and her innocent exclamations of joy when she saw it. It's that sense that a Maserati is the car that's like a Ferrari, only rarer, and posher. It's that faint suggestion, in the sawn-off rump, of a modern, Italian and electronically sophisticated version of James Bond's DB5.

I suppose our feelings for cars are like our feelings for music, or what we find beautiful in a member of the opposite sex. It's all to do with some forgotten association, some childish memory. That is why I felt so fine as I drove at speeds I do not think I should disclose, humming to myself those bars from wizened old rocker Joe Walsh: 'My Maserati does 185. I've lost my licence so now I can't drive.' That's why I ran my fingers so reverentially over the oxblood leather. Thank you, *GQ*, thank you, I whispered when I got home and opened the bonnet; and like those hunting types who blood themselves in the warm guts of the poor dead brute, I suddenly wanted to run my fingers lovingly over the engine, caressing the embossed black trident designed by Mario Maserati and inspired by Giambologna's statue of Neptune. 'Yowch,' I said. Reverentially.

BORIS AND THE

SEX BOMB

Our motoring guru has to make a choice between his political career and a Porsche Carrera.

I'll tell you one thing about being a top-flight motoring correspondent like me: it's hard on our emotions. It's the promiscuity. It's the one-night stands. It's the endless weekends with different partners.

Oh, I bet you won't respect me if I say I get involved with some of the cars I handle. I know why you come to this column: for the curling-lipped disc-brake analysis, the cool camshaft appraisal. This is where you get the technical poop that even Clarkson misses, the hard-headed stuff about the torque and the cormthrusters, not forgetting the sarcastic adjectives, the caustic asides, the sprinkling of desperate sexual metaphors.

And you are right. After more than a year of testing cars for the *GQ* readership I think I am starting to know my superchargers from my crabbing pins. But there are times when the carapace of my professionalism is penetrated. Sometimes I fall for a car and succumb to the curse of the muttering rotter, as we motoring writers self-deprecatingly describe ourselves.

One minute you're caressing her leather, you're whimpering as she gives you the ride of your life, and then, just as you are approaching a climax of enthusiasm, she's taken away from you. The car's PR people ring up *GQ*, and that's it. You're wrenched apart by fate and all you can do is look back through tear-fringed eyes.

There we are at the outset of the weekend, me and the Porsche 911. She knows what I want and in the words of Tom Jones' 'Sex Bomb' – an ingenious song which combines in its title the two English words most widely understood by the world's population – baby, I can turn her on. Yes, baby, I can turn her on.

Actually it took some time to work out how to do this, but once I'd remembered the trick with the foot brake, I turned her on and in no time we were roaring away, two hearts with but a single thought, two minds that beat as one.

My gorgeous new acquaintance was all but turned into a squashed sardine tin, with me in the role of sardines.

Me and the 911, we were like that. Actually, we were almost like that, in that my gorgeous new acquaintance was all but turned into a squashed sardine tin, with me in the role of sardines, when we came into High Wycombe so fast that I sort of forgot about the roadworks.

'Oh baby,' I breathed to the machine when she ceased to waggle her lovely silver hips and returned to the straight and narrow of the contraflow, and my brow was dewed with an ecstasy of relief; and I think it even possible that I snogged the airbag sign.

My mission that day was to attend a fair in a lovely Oxfordshire village, and you know what? I felt embarrassed to show her off there. I don't normally feel I've anything to hide. I've made it perfectly clear to my putative constituency association that I have this lifestyle, with a string of ever more glamorous and exotic cars.

Sometimes you fall for a car … I think I snogged the airbag.

And as we all know, the Tory party is changing fast. They understand that Britain has moved on from the mores of the Fifties, and that a chap can roll up with a different set of car keys in his hand every month. They are polite enough not to mention it, but as we thrummed through Watlington and I felt eyes turn towards us as my baby emitted Porsche noises through the great flues of her rump, I sort of flunked it.

No, I thought, I'm not going to turn up at a fair, where the nicest people in the world are selling cakes and half-broken toys, with one of the most sensual cars in the world. Nope, I said to myself: they'll look up from the trestles of begonias and see my motor, and think, hooker, tart, strumpet. This car, in their eyes, is going to be the automotive equivalent of a Venezuelan *poule de luxe*. They won't understand that she's not mine, that I'm just road-testing her.

I'm damn well going to avoid the confusion, I said, and I *arumarumarummed* through the village without stopping, yanked the wheel to the left, shot up a farm track and slid into a ditch.

I got out, and my eyes met those of a woman watching me from her front path. Did she know that this was her would-be MP? I walked on, whistling, and felt her gaze on my back.

What was she thinking? Did she disapprove? Or was she just puzzled at the sight of someone parking £65,000 of German *wunderwagen* in a ditch and then pretending it was nothing to do with him? Oh, I don't know and, frankly, how pathetic that I should care.

Why should I mind what the world thinks? Our time together was far too brief to worry about that kind of thing. Because the following morning she was gone for ever, snatched back by Alex, the *GQ* features supremo. In a fit of sentimentality, I have just bought a magazine called *911 & Porsche World* to remind me of her.

Of course I can't buy a 911; but perhaps I could buy one of these accessories as a keepsake: these brake-cooling ducts for £54.99 per pair, perhaps. Ah no: here we are. Leopardskin mirror bras for £39.95 per pair. That's my baby.

Vital statistics

In January 2001 Porsche unveiled a 200mph version of the 911, called the GT2. Just 300 will be built, priced around £100,000.

Engine 3.4-litre 24V flat six, 296bhp
Performance 175mph, 0–60mph in 5.2 secs
Price (2001) £55,950

BAVARIAN RHAPSODY

BMW's fabulous new X5 goes head-to-head with the 4x4 establishment.

This month I want to talk about vanity or, to give it the psychologists' name, cognitive dissonance. From puberty we human beings kid ourselves about the way we look. When our chins first sprout hair, we imagine it will be read as a sign of virility, a butch sort of shagginess, whereas everyone else sees horrible bum-fluff and spots. We see the miraculous flowering of our chick-magnet chest muscles; the chicks see puppy fat. So it goes on through life, a refusal to reconcile self-image with reality.

When, like me, you enter your late middle youth, you still think of yourself as you were at 20 – a lithe, athletic 14-stone hunk. It's the snapshot you store in your mental wallet. So when you are walking down the road and you pass a reflecting window, you do a double-take.

'Christ,' you think, in an absent-minded sort of way, 'who is that fat geezer with the lined face and the elephant suit, and the glazed, hungover look? Wait, no, it can't be …' And you turn aside and you dismiss the apparition as a trick of the light, and you console yourself by whipping out that mental self-image. Of course you do, because the self-image is always pristine and glossy and suave, and every year the reality decays, like the picture of Dorian Gray.

To understand what I am getting at, perhaps it would be helpful to compare two vehicles. In the new BMW X5 monster *Krautwagen*, you see my ideal self: still very much a family machine, oh yes, but sensationally fast. It is a muscle car with enough room for a Labrador, or a couple of kiddies' bikes. Yes, the new BMW *über-*Range Rover is just the kind of car I'd like to be. If you were a psychologist and you were trying to help me with my problems, and you said, 'Boris, imagine you are a car. What kind would you like to be?' I would answer without hesitation. 'I'd like to be the snazzy, boxy super-cool BMW four-wheel-drive *strudelpanzer*,' I'd blurt. 'In fact, I rather like to think that in terms of aspiration and achievement, where I am in the world, and so on, that car sums me up.'

The new BMW *über*-Range Rover is just the sort of car I'd like to be.

And there, my friends, you have the vanity of our species, the relentless self-deception with which we protect our common frailty. Because when other people see me driving along, they do not see a man in a shiny Beemer, hunkered high on all-weather Michelins as thick as your midriff. They see the reality: that I possess a clapped-out six-year-old Toyota Previa DL.

When I think of myself, I think of the Beemer, the 20–20 vision of the oxyacetylene blue headlamps slicing the dark for miles in advance. The awful truth is that I am really the Toyota, puffed up and staggering half-blind, the windscreen dewed with a permanent fog.

The BMW X5 is the kind of car that has the guys on Holloway Road rolling down the windows of their Isuzu pick-ups and displaying non-ironic signs of ecstasy. It is a car you can take somewhere posh: Ascot, or some luxury country house weekend, where everyone turns out as the scrunching gravel announces your arrival, and the ice rattles in the girls' gin and tonics. The Toyota, on the other hand, is so distressed, with a hubcap missing like a front tooth, that anyone else would hide it in the bushes and walk the rest of the drive.

The BMW X5 is the kind of car that has guys in pick-ups rolling down their windows to display non-ironic signs of ecstasy.

In the BMW's acceleration, in the cleanness and the silence, I see the athleticism of the old days; in the sogginess of the Toyota you see the miserable truth about me, and legs that could no longer carry me 100 metres in 12 seconds. It is not too much to say that in the Beemer's lustrous dashboard you see my face as I imagine it: simple, honest and smooth. The Previa gives you the reality: a fascia cracked and stained with coffee, yoghurt, and various bodily fluids.

They are both big cars, but the X5 is a

lean, fit, hungry, washboard-stomached kind of car. The Previa, apparently named after a childbirth complication called *placenta previa*, is a great big fat mobile advertisement for vasectomy.

There you have it, my faithful friends, you faithful few who have stuck with me almost to the end of this article. That is the difference between my self-image and the reality. It is the difference between a lovely new BMW and a Jap peoplewagon of a certain age. Every day the memory of my X5 grows fainter and every day it grows harder to remember exactly what it felt like to sit in those soft, young kidskin seats. And all the while the reality of the aged Previa, with its spilt McDonald's slurry sauce, grows daily more oppressive.

What consolations do we have, the Previa and I, as we career off the motorway of life, and rattle down lanes that are ever darker and damper and colder, until we are finally crushed together, image and reality, somewhere on the scrapheap of history? Good question. I don't know. Perhaps there are no consolations, as we all make the transition from Beemer to Previa. Oh no, wait a mo. I'll tell you one advantage of the Previa: it has a much better turning circle than the *Krautwagen*.

Suppose both cars were trapped in some great natural disaster, and the Previa and the BMW had to do a three-point turn – I reckon the Previa would be the first to turn its back on the oncoming torrent of lava.

There; I don't know how it fits into my self-image/reality metaphor, but that must be good news of some kind.

Vital statistics

The X5 is BMW's first foray into the lucrative luxury SUV market.

Engine 4.4-litre, 32V V8, 286bhp
Performance 128mph, 0–60mph in 7.3 secs
Price (2001) £44,670

'I'M OUT OF PETROL!'

Ferrari's 456M GTA punishes our man's thriftiness.

Anyone who has sat at the wheel of a Ferrari will know the feeling. You look at the other cars piddling along, with their lawnmower engines and their bourgeois safety features, and you know that you are the king of the road. You look at the black horse prancing on the yellow shield between your hands; you listen to the music of the mighty motor, and you know that you have arrived.

It may not, strictly speaking, be your Ferrari; you may simply be testing it for a magazine. But one way or another you have shoe-horned yourself into the leather seat of £176,000 worth of Italian engineering genius, and you feel an understandable sense of invulnerability. For four days I test-drove the Ferrari 456M GTA. I whanged it down to Taunton on Friday afternoon, gave a speech, and whomped it back to London before lights-out. I twanged it round the villages of south Oxfordshire, and noted the magnificent disdain with which it took the corners. And perhaps because this 456

The 456 is inspired by Ferrari's classic Daytona grand tourer.

has an automatic transmission, and perhaps because I couldn't quite get over my apparent skill in handling one of the world's most powerful production cars, I am ashamed to say that I became complacent.

Readers of *GQ*, you high-income bracket thrusters and potential Ferrari drivers, learn from my misfortune. The black horse is a demanding god. He cannot be taken for granted. It was about 6.15pm as I left the offices of the *Spectator* for an engagement

The great V12 Ferrari engine makes a sound like a stallion kept too long in winter quarters.

in Oxfordshire, and I calculated that I had plenty of time. The car burbled into life, and we nosed out through Holborn towards the Marylebone Road. Now, one of the features of the Ferrari, as you will have noticed if you have watched one in traffic, is that it has no small talk. The great V12 Ferrari engine does not putter harmoniously along, in unison with all the other lesser machines. As it bucks and lurches forward, it makes a kind of frustrated bellow, like a stallion kept too long in winter quarters. Normally, this would not have troubled me, except that a dashboard sign had suddenly lit up. It was the biggest such sign that I have seen on any car. It showed a red petrol pump.

I don't know about you, but I'm not a petrol panicker. When my car says it wants more fuel, I am pretty relaxed. Most cars these days are rather like Parker pen cartridges, in that they seem to have a big reserve tank. Such is my sang-froid that I am capable of driving for 30 miles with the empty tank light flickering ever more emphatically. All the same, I will not conceal from you that I felt the tiniest vibration of alarm.

Do you know how many petrol stations there are on the way out to the M40 from the Marylebone Road, once you have overshot that stygian little CYMA place? Neither did I. The answer is zero, and by the time we panted our way to the first traffic lights after the Westway flyover, my apprehension was rising. How many litres could there be left, if we had travelled five miles since the warning sign went on? It all depended on how thirsty a Ferrari is.

I'd last filled it up on the M4, and was so stunned by the spooling digits of the pump – and realising that I'd probably forget to bill it to this magazine – that I gave up, in a stupor, before the tank was full. So I already suspected that the Ferrari was a bit of a drinker, getting through the gasoline with all the ruthlessness of Pavarotti handling a plate of pasta.

I sort of knew, in my bones, that there was a limit to its willingness to roar and howl at 5mph, while all 12 cylinders were slurping down their ration, and I started to make plans for disaster. The mobile phone: that was the first and most important thing. The mobile phone was not in the anorak pocket. If it was anywhere, it was probably on my desk five miles away. Oh come on, I told myself. This car isn't going to conk out on you. You've been here before, I told myself, and every time you have limped into the garage, with all the tearful jubilation of a World War II bomber, back from Bremerhaven with its tank shot away, pancaking blissfully at Biggin Hill.

The Ferrari was a bit of a drinker, getting through the gasoline with all the ruthlessness of Pavarotti handling a plate of pasta.

Vital statistics

Engine 5.5.-litre 48V V12, 434bhp
Performance 187mph, 0–62mph in 5.2 secs
Price (2001) £176,233

Nonetheless, it has to be admitted that this traffic was pretty glacial; and I was starting to work out how I could get in touch with my friend in Oxfordshire when, without any preamble or clearing of the throat, my brand-new Ferrari came to a halt. We had come to rest in the fast lane of the A40 at White City, and a road already congested became so blocked that I imagine we were a subject of immediate comment by Capital Radio's flying eye. No, no, no, I said, wrenching my hair and turning the key again. Perhaps we have just stalled.

There is a computer aboard the Ferrari which goes beep, beep, beep, beep while it checks that everything is all right, before it allows you to turn on the engine. Check OK, said the dashboard. But another sign said check engine. There was nothing for it. There was no hiding the reality. I want to thank first of all the nice woman with the Alfa Spider who let me use her mobile. I want to thank the police, who turned up after 45 of the most stressful minutes of my life, while enraged commuters slewed past me, honking and howling their abuse. Both officers were immensely charitable, and pushed me off the road without asking any questions.

I also want to thank the man who gave me a V-sign as he passed, and, leaning out, shouted, 'Johnson, you ****!' It was no more than I deserved.

FOR THE EMPEROR!

Our blue-rinse kamikaze steps behind the wheel of a Mitsubishi Evo for his latest mission.

It was more than half a century ago that the flower of Japanese youth clambered into their Mitsubishis, donned their goggles and prepared to die for the emperor. They called them the kamikaze pilots, a word deriving from *kami* (divine) and *kaze* (wind), and reflecting their belief that they were the agents of cosmic retribution. They tied on their colourful headscarves. They said their prayers to their ancestors. In front of them, the ground-crew lollipop men did their sign language for the last time. The Mitsubishi Zeros nosed towards the end of the aircraft carrier, turned around to face the other way, accelerated down the deck and took off towards the hated Americans.

'Banzai!' they cried – which is Japanese for tally-ho – and wobbled through the sky, their noses so laden with explosives it was a miracle they ever found their targets. I think of them now as I drive this Mitsubishi Evo VI, and I wonder what technological advances are due to them and their magnificent crashes.

Oh, it has the speed, this Mitsubishi; it has all the speed of a swarm of suicidal Zeros coming in out of the sun and raining down on the deck of some vast American aquatic fortress. This car is clearly designed as a sort of rebuke, a crushing rejoinder from Mitsubishi to the souped-up Subaru Impreza reviewed in this column previously, and there is no doubt that it pings up the hills of the M40 with terrific power and verve.

The Evo has all the speed of a swarm of Zeros coming out of the sun.

Just touch that throttle and listen to the sweet moan, and watch the rev counter undulate to and fro, like the loose kimono of a geisha flapping in the afternoon breeze around 5.30pm, when the tea ceremony is finished and there isn't much to do except a spot of calligraphy or rehearsing some of the ancient arts of pleasing a man with unguent of jasmine. And yes, this car has all the luxury one associates with a kamikaze plane – the leather seats, the air conditioning, the soft downy footwell, the groovy radio and CD player. What's that you say? Are you trying to tell me the Japanese did not bother to make the cabins of their suicide bombers especially luxurious? My friend, how little you understand of Japanese ethics and culture. These men were the chief glory of the sons of Nippon. Don't tell me their wives and girlfriends didn't make sure their final moments were spent in comfort. I can't tell you exactly what kit they had in their cockpits, since many of the planes are in small pieces at the bottom of the sea, but I can tell you it was more than a box of Kleenex on the back seat.

The Mitsubishi surges like one of the vast £60,000 silver tuna that weave through Tokyo bay.

And then there is one final reason why I feel at home in this four-wheeled inheritor of the great kamikaze tradition: I know, very dimly, how those men felt. What were they doing but laying down their lives and happiness for their country? They were making a terminal decision. Kamikaze pilots couldn't just stop their motors at the end of the carrier flight deck and announce they had this brilliant new way of serving the emperor without dying for him, such as working as a ticket collector in the Kyoto pleasure gardens.

No, whatever his inner turmoil, he bared his ribbon of teeth, clenched his fist, pulled back the throttle and shouted, 'Tora! Tora! Tora!' And the reason I know how he felt is that I too have taken a step that means the end of my life as I know it. By the time you read this article, I will be figuratively airborne and heading towards the New

Labour fleet on a mission to destroy, and the battle cry on my lips will be 'Tory! Tory! Tory!'

I do not know how it will end. But I feel in my bones the impact of the coming collision. Now the Mitsubishi surges along through the traffic like one of the vast £60,000 silver tuna fish, all muscle, that escape the harpoon by weaving through the fishing boats in Tokyo bay. And now the traffic is gone and I let the throttle open up, and we fizz along in fine style.

Which is it to be? Death or glory? Or both? Or neither? Here is a thought for all of us who await the new Parliament. Of course, we are all entitled to mourn our careers as editors and top-flight car reviewers. But it would be even worse if we were somehow to fail. What if our explosives decline to go off, and we bounce absurdly on the fo'c's'le of the enemy ship? What if we have no alternative but to get out, pretend that nothing has happened and get on with our former careers? There was no higher disgrace as a kamikaze pilot than trying to commit suicide and failing. Nope, that's one thing you don't want on your CV. 2001: Kamikaze pilot (failed).

Vital statistics

The Mitsubishi Evo VI Tommi Makinen Edition is modelled on World Rally Champion Tommi Makinen's own Group A Lancer.

Engine 2.0-litre 16V turbo four, 276bhp
Performance 150mph, 0–62mph in under 5 secs
Price (2001) £32,995

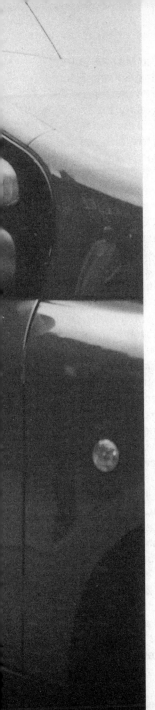

ANY COLOUR YOU LIKE AS LONG AS IT'S BLUE

To keep the red menace from overrunning Henley, Boris looks to Europe and woos the voters with the help of a comfortingly Continental Fiat Multipla.

Think yourself back to May 28, 2001, about a week before the General Election. The polls looked bad. If I understood the numbers correctly, my party, the Tories, the most successful political party of the last 200 years, was about to melt down and disintegrate like the baddies at the end of *Raiders of the Lost Ark*. Even in south Oxfordshire, where I was standing for election, I was experiencing the first pricklings of paranoia. Could I lose? Could I blow the majority accumulated by Michael Heseltine?

That very morning a transvestite had threatened to run me over. A transvestite! Did she not grasp that the Tories were nothing if not the party of diversity, choice and transvestism? Another man had told me to hop it, and when one woman answered my knock, she took one look at me, screamed and slammed the door in my face. We laughed, of course, as we marched on to the next doorstep, but it was hollow laughter. We knew we needed a piece of luck, an intervention from on high; and there, when we returned to the office at lunchtime, it was.

Now, I will not hide it from you that there was controversy at our HQ when we saw the car *GQ* had sent us. 'Call that a battlewagon?' said someone (it might have been me). It looked more like the car the Ant Hill Mob drives in *Wacky Races*. It appeared to be some kind of Fiat, with a bulge around the middle of its frontal parts, like a roll of fat, or a broken nose, or a double chin. It seemed self-consciously eccentric, and we weren't sure, frankly, what effect it would have on the voters.

The colour was good; the colour was fine. It was a deep Conservative cerulean blue, like Mrs Thatcher's dresses during her *Gloriana Imperatrix* phase. It was as blue, in fact, as the nose of a south Oxfordshire colonel after he has laughed immoderately at a sally in the *Daily Telegraph* leader, and choked on his Shreddies. No, I had no problem with the colour, but I did worry about the tone, the ethos, of the machine.

The colour was a deep Conservative cerulean blue, like Mrs Thatcher's dresses during her *Gloriana Imperatrix* phase.

There would be those who thought it flash; there would be those who thought it foreign; and there would be those who thought a Tory candidate in a rural seat should be driving around in a Land Rover and nothing else. But what could we do? Our position was grave, if not yet hopeless. We knew, as we studied the polls, that we must take a risk.

So we plastered the Fiat in Tory election stuff and set off in the general direction of the voters. Nothing much happened at first as we cruised through the countryside. They say that spring rain does wonders for hawthorn, and the blossom hung like snow upon the hedgerows. Every lawn was a masterpiece, as carefully shaved as William Hague's buzzcut.

We could have driven happily for hours, in fact, goggling at nature from the elevated seats. Sooner or later, however, we were bound to come across a member of the electorate, and then we would know. Then we would know how the average Oxfordshire voter felt about our car and our last-ditch bid for popularity.

The voters either liked my name on the side or they liked the car. The Fiat was a hit!

Vital statistics

The Fiat Multipla JTD105ELX has three-abreast seating for six people.

Engine 1.9-litre 8V four-cylinder diesel
Performance 107mph, 0–62mph in 12.2 secs
Price (2001) £15,894

As it happened, we did not see him. We heard him. We heard a sudden hooting, and someone overtook us. He was raising his fist. Was he giving us a V-sign? Was he telling us where to go? My friends, he was giving us the thumbs up! And then there was more hooting, and more friendly gestures, or gestures that were at worst ambiguous. They either liked my name on the panels or they liked the car. It didn't matter. The thing was a hit. All my reservations fell away.

Even if the suspension was a bit rocky – so what? Didn't that prove one of the core slogans of my campaign: that the roads of south Oxfordshire were a disgrace, and that every pothole was a Liberal Democrat pothole? I played with the electric windows, partly for the hell of it and partly because we had a very nice Japanese journalist on board who had eaten a lot of raw fish and garlic. And so for a week we drove the curious cuboid Fiat around the constituency, and were received with good humour and indulgence, until the night of June 7, when we parked it at the count in Watlington.

It may have been a bad night for the Tories, but it was a good night in Henley. I cannot say that the car was wholly responsible, but I cannot rule out the possibility that it helped.

RELIGIOUS CONVERT(IBLE)

Our albino-haired agent and his Saab take a stand against fundamentalism.

Now, when you get into the hot seat of this gorgeous little Saab, I want you to forget all embarrassment. Never mind that it looks vaguely like a boat, with a big rubber fender at the front and back. Never mind that you suspect it's the kind of car that might be driven by a record executive, or your old man as he cruises into his fourth midlife crisis.

To drive the Saab 9-3 Aero is an exultant affirmation of everything we stand for here at *GQ*: capitalism, consumerism, freedom, and the ability to drive slightly too fast with a girl in your lap, one hand on the wheel and the other in her hair. It's about choice, democracy, habeas corpus, an independent judiciary, and everything the Islamic mullahs hate and fear about western civilisation. How do I know this? I will tell you.

The other day I was bowling up Doughty Street, home of the *Spectator*, when I saw my old chum Alexei Sayle, the renowned Marxist thinker. Like all Marxists these days, Alexei is an unrepentant materialist. (Incidentally, he drives a big eggshell-coloured 3-litre Alfa 166 that is always conking out with electrical problems, and which he offered to sell me for £15,000. That's why he's known as a satirist.) Alexei knows about most cars, and he told me a fascinating little thing about my Saab convertible. This design, he said, has been basically unchanged for about 20 years, and many famous people have owned cars like the one I am pictured in today. What literary historians have too often forgotten is the identity of the distinguished man who bought a Saab convertible back in 1988.

He was already a Booker Prize-winning author; he had a scraggly bum-fluff beard; he had hooded eyes, and was always writing whingeing stuff saying what a dump Britain was under Margaret Thatcher. That's right, folks: it was Salman Rushdie! And do you know what – said Alexei – that purchase was almost the last thing Salman did as a free man in this country. Because within days the Ayatollah Ruhollah Khomeini had apparently launched a formal fatwa against him, promising all faithful Muslims that if they killed Rushdie they would be guaranteed a Club Class place in heaven.

Within days, mobs of Asians in Bradford were pelting WHSmith and shouting 'Kill Rushdie!' The Rugby-educated wordsmith was whisked away into a safe place; the British taxpayer began to cough up for his protection, to the tune of about a million a year; and the Saab – the symbol of his lost freedom – was left to rust, unused in the garage like a caged tiger. Now everyone has always believed that the Ayatollah's wrath was inspired simply by his reading of Salman's latest novel, *The Satanic Verses*, which was allegedly blasphemous against Islam. This theory has always seemed to me to have one yawning implausibility. Have you ever struggled through one of Mr Rushdie's books to the end? Neither have I, and neither, I bet, had the Ayatollah. In any case, do you really think that this old beardie wanted to have Rushdie bumped off just because of a few gags in some pretentious novel? It's just incredible, and thoroughly unlikely, isn't it?

And as soon as Alexei let fall this nugget about Rushdie buying the Saab, it all fell into place. Imagine the Ayatollah, sitting there in the city of Qom. The women are veiled from head to toe, and the men are flagellating themselves quietly with wooden blocks. Then a yelp pierces the calm of the cloister, and the motes of dust twitch in the afternoon sun. It is the Ayatollah, who has spotted a picture of Rushdie in the Peterborough column of the *Daily Telegraph*. 'Blasphemy man buys new car' is the headline, and there's a picture of Rushdie with the Saab.

'By the beard of the prophet!' croaks the Ayatollah, hurling the paper from him. 'Son of a mangy dog! May the fleas of a thousand camels infest his armpits!' And seeing their spiritual and political leader in such a lather, the other mullahs gather round nervously, stroking their typewriter-shaped beards.

'Look at the blasphemer Rushdie and his disgusting capitalist materialist car, built in Sweden, but owned by Americans, the servants of Shaitan!' cries the enraged Ayatollah. 'Let the word go forth – destroy Rushdie's Saab!' And, of course, the mullahs immediately take up the chant, scourging

Vital statistics

Engine 2.0-litre turbo, 205bhp
Performance 127mph, 0–60mph in 8.1 secs
Price (2001) £31,995 approx

themselves with prayer beads and calling: 'Destroy Rushdie's Saab!'

Alas, the mobs in Lahore and Islamabad have never heard of a Saab convertible. The mission to 'Destroy Rushdie's Saab' soon becomes 'Destroy Rushdie Sahib,' which is shortened, within hours, to 'Kill Rushdie!' And that, I conjecture, is how the fatwa spread worldwide.

I feel strongly that this car stands for the things we cherish in western civilisation.

Within less than a week WHSmith has withdrawn the book, and thousands of Muslims are vowing to prosecute the most demented plan to kill a blasphemer since the Middle Ages. And all because of a mix-up between the homophones Saab and Sahib. That is why I feel so strongly that this car stands for the things we cherish in western civilisation: liberty, democracy, ice cream Mars Bars – everything they have tried to stamp out in the crazed theocracy that is modern Iran.

We may not think much of Rushdie. We may not be able to get through his books. In fact, if the mobs in Bradford choose to burn them, we may warm our hands by the blaze. But we defend absolutely his right to write them, and we defend to the death his right to drive a Saab convertible, whatever the Ayatollah says.

THE LANCASHIRE LAMBORGHINI

Sticks of rock, false breasts and sports cars … Boris samples yet another fine Blackpool export – TVR's Tamora.

When I tumbled out of the front seat of the TVR Tamora, I was jangling all over like a drill. My tongue clove to the roof of my mouth. My eyeballs oscillated like things that oscillate a lot. Ocelots, perhaps. I was sweating. I was tired. And those parts of the brain which supply adjectives to motoring correspondents were all seized up with the wrong sort of hormone. My word, I said to myself, that car is, um … It's, er … It's fast.

Yes, of course it's fast, said my inner literary critic. It has a 3.6-litre straight-six engine, like all the classic British sports cars of the 20th century. It can attain a speed of 60mph in less than four seconds and a top speed of 170mph. It's fast, all right, but you are being paid to come up with something a bit more flowery than that.

You can't just ring up Dylan Jones and the rest of the guys at *GQ* and say, hey, chaps, guess what – the new TVR is fast.

Think of the poor benighted readers of *GQ*, said my inner literary critic. They sort of assume that this thing is fast, looking as it does like a cross between an ICBM and a particularly nasty German souped-up suppository. They want to know what it feels like to drive; they want mood, ethos, character. Above all, they want to know whether it is glamorous.

My word, I said to myself, that car is, um … It's, er … It's fast.

OK, I said to my inner literary critic; I get the point. And I looked hard at the car again; and I frowned, and tried to think of some other means of describing the machine. It's fast, rapid, quick, a bit of a mover; it covers the distance between A and B with alacrity, celerity and velocity …

Oh to hell with it, I thought; and in search of inspiration I rang TVR's own Ben Samuelson to discover just how glamorous this car really was. And I must confess that to begin with, my researches were not encouraging.

Take the very name, TVR. You might expect that these three letters stood for something almost erotically glamorous, just as GTV stands for Gran Turismo Veloce. But no, it turns out that it is an abbreviation of the old English Christian name Trevor, since the TVR company was founded by a man called Trevor in 1947.

You mean, I said, just to be sure I had heard correctly, that TVR just stands for Trevor?

'Yeah,' said Ben, the man from TVR, gloomily. 'There was Enzo Ferrari. There was Ferruccio Lamborghini. And there was Trevor Wilkinson.'

Right, I said. And where do they make them, these cars called Trevor? Where is the spiritual home of the TVR?

'Er, in Lancashire,' said Ben in a guarded sort of way.

I tried to think of a glamorous part of Lancashire. Whereabouts? I asked.

'Blackpool, actually,' said Ben.

Well, folks, Blackpool is commonly agreed to have many attributes, but glamour is not among them. In fact, in a hotly contested field, it is the most vulgar place in Britain.

Some of us spend at least a part of every autumn in Blackpool during the party conference season, and at the end of each conference, there is a little competition among the journalists. Everyone goes out to buy something from the wares of Blackpool, and the winner is the person who can find the most embarrassing object.

You may not believe this, but for some reason almost every shop in Blackpool seems to specialise in enormous false breasts, or six-foot long 'joke' willy warmers, or hilarious plastic dog turds. Every year the journalists parade these objects and their snobby southern eyes run with tears of laughter. One year, I remember, the top

Vital statistics

The Tamora is TVR's 'softest' car – but it still lacks ABS, airbags and traction control.

Engine 3.6 litre straight-six, 350bhp
Performance 170mph, 0–60mph in under 4.0 secs
Price (2002) £36,500

prize went to a wind-up toy which mechanically enacted the love that flowers between a woman and a German shepherd dog.

Such, at any rate, are the objects which I have normally taken to be emblematic of Blackpool, and that is why I gasped when Ben from TVR told me of the machine's provenance.

It was an honour to drive a car which manages so magnificently to overcome its background.

'Blackpool?' I said.

'Yup,' said Ben; and I put down the telephone rather in the same mood as I had got out of the car – breathless and stunned.

I looked again at the machine, still sizzling and smoking from our death-ride up the M40 and back. From its vast engine – entirely made in Blackpool; Blackpool through and through like a stick of rock – there came pinking noises. And then I gave it another little spin round the block and marvelled again at the way it stuck to the corners as though they were tram-tracks. I gawped again at the acceleration, which thumps you in the back with all the vehemence of a Tory whip who sees you accidentally walking into the 'Ayes' lobby by mistake.

I looked at the funny little knob under the wing mirror, which you use to open the doors. And this time I saw not a clumsy piece of design. I saw a brilliant anti-theft device.

I saw how utterly trivial my objections were. Who cares if the car is made in Blackpool? Who cares if it is named after a man called Trevor? As the Duke of Wellington pointed out to the historian who noted that he was born in a stable in Dublin, that did not make him a horse. It was an honour to drive a car which manages so magnificently to overcome its background, to shake off its curious abbreviated name.

The TVR roars like an old Aston, or an Austin-Healey; and yet with modern engine management it goes twice as fast and it doesn't oil its plugs at the traffic lights.

As Ben says, and he will refund you if he is wrong: 'It's quicker than anything else for the money.' That's the Tamora for you. They say Tamora never comes. But she certainly goes.

THE IRON-ON LADY

Boris transfers his allegiances on to the roof of a Mini Cooper S.

'OK,' I said. 'Groovy,' I said. Every so often
the style gurus and stunt merchants of the
GQ car department come up with a real
snorter of an idea, and the only course is to
snap to attention.

'It's gonna be brilliant,' said Tim Lewis,
the automobile supremo. 'We get this new
Mini Cooper S, a fantastic car, a real
monster car, and we superimpose a picture
on the roof!'

'Tremendous, Tim,' I exclaimed, because
it is important to humour one's bosses, 'and
whose image are you proposing? Saddam
Hussein?'

'Close,' said Lewis, 'but no cigar. You're
going down to the Tory party conference,
aren't you? Well, you are about to be the
most popular MP there. You will find blue-
rinse matrons blubbing and patting your
flanks. Acnoid Tory boys with sterling-silver
"Keep The Pound" badges are going to be
licking your hubcaps, Boris. Because we are
going to decorate your car in glorious,
pouting Technicolor with a six-foot,
two-and-a-half times life-size rotogravure

photo-image of … Margaret Thatcher!'

'Tim,' I said weakly, closing my eyes to steady my nerves, 'that is one hell of a wheeze.' And over the next few days, as I waited for the car to arrive, I tried to persuade myself that it would, indeed, be a cinch to carry it off.

'Yeah, well?' I would say, if anyone asked me what the hell I thought I was doing with a picture of Maggie on the roof. Why shouldn't a British car pay homage to the woman who revived our motor industry, by the wise expedient of flogging it off to the Japanese and the Germans? Maybe Tim was right. Maybe it was about time we Tories started sticking up for Maggie and her legacy, and stopped leaving Blair to lay claim to all that was best in her inheritance.

I had just about persuaded myself that it was a runner, when She arrived. 'Fantastic!' I stammered, as Tim unveiled the Mini Thatcher.

She was in her *Gloriana Imperatrix* mode, in a deep-indigo dress, hands folded royally in her lap and covered with bling-bling. Her hair was immaculately bouffed, not its normal pineapple chunks colour, but more marmalade-ish, like bronze-lacquered strands of shredded wheat.

She looked terrific. In terms of motor car iconography, she was a major statement. But could she really be risked in public? If you went on *Question Time*, and said Maggie Thatcher had done a lot of good for the country, the audience would howl and curse, scratching and hooting like flea-ridden gibbons. Oh, Maggie, baby, I thought once Tim had left, how can I do this to you?

They'll scratch you with key rings. They'll shake their fists.

Across Britain, sour-faced, taxpayer-funded politics lecturers are teaching the young that Thatcher was a vile shrew, who encouraged selfishness and greed, who destroyed our manufacturing industry, who denied the very existence of society. Of course it is all lies, but what do they know, the youth of today? Overcome by funk, I decided to do something I had never done before. I disobeyed Tim.

She was in regal mode, in an indigo dress, hands folded and covered in bling-bling.

I hid the Maggiemobile in an underground car park in London's Russell Square, and went to Bournemouth by train. That night, though, something spooky happened. As I lay in my hotel, I thought I heard a voice calling in the dark, a low, breathy contralto. 'It's a funny old world,' said the Maggiemobile from the dark of the garage. 'They all betrayed me: Heseltine, Hurd, Patten – and now you, too, Boris. Why won't you drive me? Are you frightened? Are you frit?' It went on for hours, and after two nights, I could take it no longer.

I returned to London and rushed to the garage. She was all right. No one had touched her or scraped her. I caressed her

Vital statistics

Engine 1,598cc, four cylinders, 16 valves, supercharged, 163bhp at 6,000rpm
Performance 135mph, 0–60mph in 7.2 secs
Fuel Economy 33.6mpg
Price (2003) from £14,500

shiny hindquarters, as cerulean blue as a Tory conference platform. And was it my imagination, or did her smile look especially regal tonight? I turned her on, and she barked her approval, with that splendid, full-throated noise that so embarrassed and frightened Howe, Gilmour, Pym and the Wets. Soon we were heading to Bournemouth, with all the British-made vigour and confidence of the Task Force heading for the Falklands.

My date was a black-tie awards dinner for 600 tax-collectors (I get some pretty hot gigs, you have to admit), and I was seriously late. But, boy, can that Maggiemobile shift. It seemed incredible, as she whanged and weaved through the rush-hour traffic, that she had only a 1.6-litre engine. I discovered that she had six forward gears, and at one point I was doing 70 in second, not entirely by mistake.

Heaven knows how fast we were going, when, somewhere along the M25, we hurtled round a corner into a wall of cars. There were red tail lights everywhere. It was brake or die. And the Maggiemachine showed the gift for self-preservation that kept her in power for an amazing 11 years. We halted. We waited. Soon I was beginning to get worried. I was meant to be the keynote speaker, and I had a sermon all ready about the joy of tax-collecting, or something of that kind.

Should I jink off at the next turning, and try to find another way to Bournemouth? And then the voice came on again in my head, as the mighty car spoke. 'You turn if you want to,' said the car, feminine and yet brimming with conviction, 'the Lady's not for turning until the junction after next!' As so often, she was right. Soon the traffic cleared; we reached the M23, turned right, and hummed down to the coast.

It was interesting, as we cruised the streets, swarming with students, to see how the world reacted to the re-emergence of Margaret Hilda Thatcher. They craned their necks to make out the picture, and then they broke out in broad grins. 'Bring back Maggie!' someone shouted, and he seemed neither old nor insane.

The following morning, having discharged my oration, I was back in London to return the car. A cowled-up black kid, not much older than eight or nine, came by on his way to school. Who's that? we asked him, pointing to the roof.

'That's the Queen,' he said, and beamed.

The cult of car 'decalcomania'

The 'Mini Thatcher' is a triumph of 'roof decalcomania,' a frankly contagious-sounding name for the process of transferring a design from a photograph on to another surface. It was pioneered by Car Vogue, a Milton Keynes-based firm which can transfer any image you like on to the roof of your car. 'Maggie is definitely the strangest decal we've been asked to do,' says Andy Pycock, who runs the company. 'We do a lot of Union Jacks, Lambretta-style targets and spider webs. But if you want to put your girlfriend, your mother or your dog on the roof, then you can do that, too.' Fortunately, if your paramour becomes a bunny boiler, or Margaret Thatcher does not go down too well in your Nottinghamshire mining constituency, then the image can be removed in a matter of minutes. And it will be fairly painless to replace: a Union Jack will cost you £180; while a fully bespoke design, like *GQ*'s Margaret Thatcher masterpiece, is a very reasonable £326.

For more info visit: www.carvogue.co.uk for a catalogue of designs.

THE REST IS HISTORY

Jaguar's X-type Sport is so comfy, it nearly cost us our car columnist …

Vital statistics

Engine 3-litre, 24V, V6, 231bhp
Performance 146mph, 0–60mph in 6.6 secs, 27.6mpg
Price £25,750

In a last-ditch attempt to keep awake, I fantasised about the headlines on the morning after the accident. Would it make the front page? A page two lead? A blob? A nib? Would I even be accorded an obituary? 'MP In Motorway Death Crash – IDS Leads Tributes.' '*GQ* Hack In Fatal Prang.' '*Spectator* Man Kicks Bucket.' And then, as the rain lashed the windscreen, I saw the truth, as if through a film of tears. What was the life of a man next to the loss of this peerless machine?

If anything, the story would be, 'Gorgeous New Jag In M4 Tragedy'. Only the most attentive reader would read on to discover that some berk had perished at the wheel. You must forgive the mawkishness, because it was 1.30am and I was driving back from addressing the Tory faithless somewhere in west Wiltshire and I was pooped. You know those pictures of squashed Red Army soldiers who got caught beneath the Panzer tracks on day one of Barbarossa? That, after a week's slogging in the Commons and running the world's greatest weekly, was how I felt.

London was more than 100 miles away, and even if I were to break the speed limit, I would have to stay awake for more than an hour. Could I? My eyelids were like a pair of maddening, ill-fitted lavatory seats: every time I forced them up, they came down again at the critical moment. I tried everything to keep awake, using all the little gizmos by which the Jag cossets its driver. I prodded the touch-sensitive electro-knobs of the air con, and turned the temperature so low, half a degree at a time, that I shivered like a man locked in a meat van. Then I tried turning it up, to roughly the temperature at which a soufflé starts to rise. Still I wanted to snooze.

The Jaguar seat has more positions than the Labour Party's education policy.

I turned the stereo so loud that it would have outraged a Brixton drug-dealer; and then I turned it right down, so quiet that I had to concentrate to catch the tune. The sound was magnificent, high or low, but still I ached for the arms of Morpheus. I tried a trick I learned on Continental motorways, of driving so fast that you scare yourself awake. It is not a clever trick, and it failed. The handling of this Jaguar X-type is so good, the 3-litre engine so deceptively powerful, that I just wasn't scared. I went

The Jaguar X-type 3.0 Sport is the first production Jaguar to feature four-wheel drive.

faster and faster in the cowhide cocoon, and still I wanted to go to sleep. It is an important physiological fact that if you start to kip at the wheel, your foot does not grow heavier on the throttle; it eases up.

And then you awake with a jerk, and you push down reflexively. Listen, I said to myself, this is madness: you are not merely endangering your own life, you are endangering the lives of anyone who is so unfortunate as to share the motorway with you. You must pull over and have 40 winks. But, at moments of crisis, we all suffer from akrasia: we know what we should do, but somehow fail to do it.

The car was so fast, and so seductive, that I persuaded myself that all was well.

You remember being in a lecture, or a tutorial, and you suddenly realise that in a minute's time you will fall asleep. The lecturer is right in front of you, and you know that it will be a total embarrassment, and you start playing all sorts of elaborate psychological tricks to keep yourself awake, usually involving sexual fantasies.

'I am awake,' you tell yourself. 'Oh yes, I am following very well, and Professor Hainsworth is talking about sex life in ancient Rome, and the curious things they did with voles. Yes, indeed, I am wide awake and being offered the sexual favours of a gorgeous, full-breasted vole. Did you say I was asleep? Nothing could be further from the truth. I am bright-eyed and bushy-tailed as the randiest vole in Rome. Here is Professor Volesworth, the most exuberant molestor of rodents in the entire faculty of *Literae Humaniores*. All voles lead to Rome. The volezzz ... Wha ... What?'

And then you realise you have just fallen asleep, woken up, and that everyone is staring. If you are driving very fast, you perform exactly the same dreadful feat of self-delusion, except that the consequences are so much more terrifying. You jolt awake just as you begin to drift from one lane to the next, and you shriek to yourself not to be such a fool.

Finally, I pulled over at Leigh Delamere. I twiddled with the seat until it was just right for a man at the end of his tether. The Jaguar seat has more positions than the *Kama Sutra*, or Labour education policy. I had promised myself only a couple of minutes, but that seat was so damn comfy that it was an hour before I awoke.

Of course there is no excuse, as I say, for running this kind of risk. The only plea I will enter in mitigation is that this car is so beguilingly tender and reverential to the driver that, *in extremis*, it really ought to be able to take over completely. I have an idea for the men at Jaguar, in case they want to help sleepyheads like me. This machine has a fantastic sat-nav system, as well as a brilliant radar that goes 'peep-peep' when you are about to bump into something. Is it really beyond the wit of man to devise a Jag that will simply steer itself, late at night, and let a man conk out? Come on, you boffins. I give it less than ten years.

ALAS, POOR REYNARD ...

When it comes to stealth and cunning, the humble fox has nothing on the new Mercedes CLK500.

Poor fox. I just can't get him out of my mind. It was 6.40am and London's Liverpool Road was empty. I had an 8am meeting in Oxfordshire, and it may be that I had decided to use a slightly bigger fraction of the power generated by the CLK. If five litres expresses the maximum thrust of the engine, then I was getting by on a thimbleful of its cubic capacity. And just before I spotted that fox – on what was to prove the last day of his life – I decided to step it up a bit.

You don't exactly gun the engine of a car like this. You just allow your right toecap to become an ounce heavier, and the thing kind of bounds. This is a car so powerful that its very exhaust pipe is as big as a letter box. Seriously, check it out: it's like a secret German weapon, with big fat lips like the muzzles of the *Bismarck*'s guns.

If this car had been made by anyone other than Mercedes-Benz, you would have heard that moment of acceleration. If this had been an Italian car, the great exhaust pipe tail gun would have barked like a howitzer, and all the windows of Liverpool Road would have rattled in their sooty casements. Across Islington, if this had been any other make, the pink-eyed pigeons would have tumbled from their love nests, and a thousand innocent dreams would have been suddenly invaded by gunshot and assassination.

But this was a Merc, among the most lovingly assembled machines you can buy. And when you change pace in a car like this, there is nothing but the soft efflatus of gas from that amazing steel orifice. It just puffs out a little more smoke, as sensually and gently as Marlene Dietrich blowing an extra smoke ring at her lover. The passer-by hears nothing. The driver hears nothing. And what haunts me is the possibility that the fox heard nothing, either.

You don't exactly gun the engine of a car like this. You just allow your right toecap to become an ounce heavier.

By the time I spotted the animal, the car was almost upon him. I had a single, thrilling glimpse of his silhouette, picked out in the icy-blue tungsten gaze of my lights. He was crossing the road in the place I had seen him before, leaving his lair in the churchyard and making for the rubbish bins in the school. He was a long, low foxy

The Mercedes CLK500 includes automatic climate control, electric front seats with memory and is all about comfort.

streak of countryside in the heart of the city, romantic, improbable.

He was not scurrying, but gliding, snout out, brush back, and he was moving fast. The question I formed then, and which haunts me now, is whether he was moving fast enough.

My friends, let us be frank: I am 99 per cent certain that he was. Thinking back, and making the relevant calculations about distance, speed and time, I cannot really credit that the Merc made any physical contact with the animal. There was no crunch, no howl, no sensation of any kind in the warm, leather-cocooned CLK.

And for the rest of the day the fox faded entirely from my thoughts, because I was wholly absorbed and happy in my job, seeing people in south Oxfordshire and trying to attend to their wishes. There were schools to visit, appeals to launch, rural pubs and post offices to defend. There were companies struggling with the burden of excessive government regulation, and who wanted to fill me in on their problems and seek my support. Some were in Henley, some were in Thame, and since mine is so large a constituency, I want to tell you how grateful I was for the Merc.

If you want a car to take the strain out of a busy day of driving, this is it. It has automatic headlamp cleaners for those muddy Oxfordshire lanes. It has an automatic steering wheel adjuster; Distronic sensors which tell you when you are about to hit another car; and a system to stop you being done for speeding. It has a Thermotronic system which means it is physically impossible for windows to steam up. It has automatic light control, automatic airbags on every side. In fact, all it lacks is an automatic letter-writer telling ministers to pull their socks up, and an automatic foxotronic system to stop you accidentally squashing little furry animals.

The CLK500 is faster than the speediest hound and more silent than the deadliest trap.

If it wasn't me, it was certainly someone. When I saw the fox again, as I drove back much later that night, he was, to be candid, looking pretty washed up. He lay in the gutter, roughly where I had last spotted him, but this time he was grey and lifeless and bedraggled. I slowed down and looked at his final rictus, the teeth that would never again kill a squirrel, or rip open your rubbish, or carry off your chickens.

'Poor fox,' I thought. 'Was it for this that you fled the terrors of the countryside? Here there are no packs of hounds, or jodhpured women on horses, or hidden gins, or farmers with their lamps and guns. Here in Islington, as long as the lefties are in charge, you will never hear the frightening "yap yap" of the huntsman's horn.'

But here, on these streets, is something more savage and more ruthless. Try as I may, I cannot entirely rule out the possibility that this fox was killed by the sheer speed and silence of the Merc. I don't think it was my car, but it has the ability to do it. The CLK is faster out of the box than the speediest hound. It is more silent than the deadliest trap. It is better upholstered than the rump of the poshest member of the Quorn or the Pytchley. More brutal even than the hunt, it may be that this car just knocked the fox, and left it to die in the gutter. I'd like to exclude the possibility that this sleek, beautiful machine is in fact the cruellest fox-killer of all. But I cannot quite rule it out. And, whichever machine is guilty, I invite the anti-hunt lobby to consider the logic of their position. Come on, you antis, and all you mushy-minded bunny-huggers: when are you going to call for a ban on cars?

Vital statistics

Engine 5-litre, V8, 306bhp
Performance 155mph (electronically limited), 0–62mph in 6 secs
Price (2003) £43,040

CHILD'S PLAY

Making the earth move turns out to be easier than Boris thought in a JCB 3CX, a luxurious vehicle whose city centre benefits have long been overlooked.

'**Hang on a bit there,** Boris,' said Mark the tester, with a note of alarm. 'There's quite a bit of weight on that, you know.' I looked out at the great yellow grovel arm as it stretched into the Staffordshire sky. Scooped in the maw of the sabre-toothed backhoe was about 26 stone of rock and mud, and the gravel dribbled from its sides, as if down the cheeks of some earth-scoffing giant.

'We don't want a flat nose, do we?' said Mark, who has been with JCB for 25 years, and who has seen some pretty inept customers in his time. 'We don't want a trip to the Staffordshire Infirmary, do we?'

'No, Mark, we don't,' I said – but the trouble was the laws of physics.

Here we were on the lip of a mud bank at the JCB test arena, ingeniously delving under the shelf on which we were standing, and somehow I'd sent the laden backhoe way out into the air. Actually, I knew how I'd done it. I was showing off to my son, the heir to the Johnson millions, and demonstrating the use of a pedal. I'd seen Mark do it. Push pedal and whoosh, the prodder extends 20 feet. I pushed.

There was a lurch, a wobble, and then everything stood still. The sun shone thin and watery on poor shivering Nigel Chell, the JCB PR man, watching about 50 yards away. I stared at the two black knobs in front of me, and tried to remember what to do. And the instant I tried to do it by intellect rather than instinct, I froze. If I did the right thing with the knobs, the great bucket would just upend itself. We would be afforded the sensual pleasure of a colossal dump, and we could all get on with the joy of shifting large quantities of earth.

Scooped in the maw of the sabre-toothed backhoe was about 26 stone of rock and mud.

If I pulled them the wrong way, then there was a risk that the whole JCB, the eight-tonne banana behemoth, would be unbalanced by the scooper and tumble forwards down the escarpment. Not only would I have to tell my wife that I'd squished our son, but totalled a brand new JCB 3CX Contractor, as well as Mark, the bobble-hatted test-driver. And if we accidentally lost Mark, what an artist would perish! He is the Nijinsky of the JCB *corps de ballet*.

This is a man who can make a JCB do push-ups, and a kind of Sydney Harbour Bridge stunt, in which all four wheels are lifted off the ground as the twin hydraulic engines make an arc of the front and back scoops. No, a mistake would be too horrible, I thought, as the wind whistled through the articulated metal diplodocus-neck. There was another creak.

'We don't want a trip to the Staffordshire Infirmary, do we?'

Was it my imagination, or did the custard colossus stir on its stanchions? The more I tried to rationalise my next move, the more I was reminded of that terrible moment when, aged 18, I was driving a large tractor in Australia. Over the months I had become accomplished at controlling this Massey Ferguson, and I was in the habit of parking it in the barn with a bit of a flourish. I would come round the corner at some speed, change down fast, brake and stop. One day I was conducting this operation when I looked down at my controls and had a complete blank. I couldn't remember what did what and drove through the back of the barn, taking the wall with me, and losing a week's salary. That is why I believe that the subconscious can save you in these moments, and I grabbed the knobs in the hope of inspiration. Right, left, up, down?

Mark was saying something about 'away from the right knee'. But which knob? It had all been going so well. We had been flown by helicopter from the Battersea Heliport, to be met at the Rocester plant by one of the many limos owned by Sir Anthony Bamford, who is among the most amiable top capitalists you will ever meet. Ivan the driver conveyed us to the site, where we were equipped with JCB hats, jackets and various histories of JCB. What a company JCB is. Alfa stands for *Anonima Lombarda Fabbrica Automobili.* Sabena stands for *Société Anonyme Belge d'Exploitation de la Navigation Aérienne.* But you know what JCB stands for? Joe Cyril Bamford.

It all began in about 1945, when Joe fitted a hydraulic loader on the front of a tractor. Brilliant! Sir Anthony is his son, the company is now dominant in 146 markets, JCB has given his initials to the language and this plant produces at least 10,000 units a year. It is one of the last triumphs of British manufacturing. As our chopper bullocked towards the landing pad, set amid lakes and landscaped greensward, I saw some interesting new orders. Parked outside the hangar was a row of olive-coloured JCBs; not cadmium yellow, but camouflage. It turns out that the Army has just bought 150. But the reason I wanted to write about JCB is that this is a machine not just for diggers or the Army, but for all of us. You can take it anywhere.

I put it to you that the JCB 3CX Contractor is the vehicle for you. It has air con, orthopaedic seats, a place you can recharge your mobile, and something called a snap box where you can keep your Mars bars. In these dark days of the New Labour tyranny, when the maniac Ken Livingstone is charging you an extra £1,200 for the privilege of using the Queen's highway, the JCB is a devastating retort. This latest model will only set you back £35,000 – cheaper than most of the cars I review.

I ask you this: when those bastards see you in the congestion zone, driving a JCB, are they going to have the guts to fine you? They are not, and if they do, just wave the monstrous tines of the front shovel in the air, and see what Livingstone does then. When urban Britain and rural Britain have had enough, when the anti-Blair revolution comes, the JCB is the instrument with which we will mount the barricades.

This JCB is not just for diggers or the Army, but it's for all of us.

That is why I came up here to learn how to do it, and until I pushed that pedal I had it sussed. Mark was kind enough to pay me a compliment. 'I've seen a lot of people do worse,' he said, as I sent one and half tonnes of rubble flying from my front loader. 'It's got a lot easier over the last 20 years,' he said. 'When I first drove these, you needed real strength for the hydraulics. Now there's no reason why a woman couldn't do it.' For the last hour, under his tuition, I had been getting better and better.

My son and I had learned to hearken to the note of the engine, straining like a sumo wrestler at stool as the front loader hefted the charge. I thought I had a feel for when to shift the knob. And now, with our lives teetering, I couldn't remember what to do. We had been digging so successfully in front of us that there seemed some possibility that the ground we were on would crumble. Which is why it was so useful to have a seven-year-old with me, because, fed up with my dithering, he seized the controls, pushed out and right.

Zonk. Clonk. Roooooooooaaaar.

No, the neck did not protract further and tilt us over the brink. Like a retching tyrannosaur the machine disgorged its mouthful. We sank back with relief. To hell with health and safety. This thing is so well made, so idiot-proof, that it can not only be operated by the weakest woman. It can not only be driven by a Tory MP. It can be handled by a competent seven-year-old.

Just to celebrate, my son and I spent the next hour moving a pile of mud from A to B And then from B to A. And back again.

Vital statistics

With two powerful excavators, damage-resistant mudguards, ergonomically designed instrumentation and the quietest cab in the business, the only drawback with the 3CX is getting it in the garage.

Engine 4-litre, 4-cylinder, 100bhp
Backhoe Max dig depth 5.46m
Loader Max lift capacity 3528kg
Weight 8070kg
Price (2003) from £35,000

LINES WRITTEN FROM A MORGAN AERO 8

Time spent with a great pillar of British motoring stirs the ode magic.

Oh God for some water, oh give me a pill.
I honestly think I'm about to be ill.
My hangover squats at the base of my skull.
My tongue is a crouton of dry cotton wool.

My brow is a raging Zambezi of sweat,
And it's hotter than hell in this barristers' set.
The sunshine is searing the back of my seat
And it saws at my neck with a sabre of heat.

I'm meant to be judging some essays in law.
But one eye is pickled; the other one's raw.
The alcohol parches the lobes of my brain
And a tramp has expired in my mid-Temple Lane.

The kids have excreted voluminous tracts,
Turgid with judgments and rigid with facts.
I burble as one who has suffered a stroke
And the wondering students assume it's a joke.

My four fellow judges have long understood
I'm rather less sharp than a blade made of wood.
Was it Article 8? Was it Article 10?
I couldn't care less and I crave Nurofen.

But out in the courtyard it's airy and mild,
And I yearn to escape like a classroom-bound child.
Dim through the glass I can hear the birds sing,
The rampant pubescence of England in spring.

The chestnut's brief candles are lovely and tall;
Beneath them the loveliest picture of all.
Out in the car park of Temple you stand
And onlookers pat you with reverent hand.

The Morgan Aero 8 has the company's signature ash frame (as strong as steel in tests).

MORGAN AERO 8

O Morgan, O Morgan, sensational car!
Just hang on and wait for me there where you are.
Your bodywork shines like the silvery pearl
In the wedding-day pin of the tie of an earl.

Each flank is a wave like a mid-ocean swell
And captured in metal as if by a spell.
Four beautiful wheels and a priest-hole to sit,
A clutch, a transmission and that's about it.

O Morgan, if ever I leave here alive
I swear we'll be off for a fabulous drive.
But wait! Dare I hope? Unless I am wrong
We've fingered the candidate fit for the gong.

Well done, mate, bravo! As I sidle outside
My hangover ebbs like a 12 o'clock tide.
I come to the car and I manage a grin.
I fish out the car keys and prise myself in.

O thrill of igniting the ultimate Morgan!
The cylinders fire like the crack of a boar-gun.
We whiz round the Temple with deafening roar,
A car out of Betjeman, Wodehouse or Waugh.

Pedestrians leap from the prow of the Morgan,
The bonnet connoting the size of my organ,
And soon we're in Oxfordshire, land of the brave
Where the natives are kind and the children behave.

The joy of the morning, the speed of the Morgan!
The white of the hawthorn, the ripening sorghum!
In Crowmarsh the people are stately and clean;
In Watlington wickedness seldom is seen.

No jealousy blooms in the path of my Morgan,
No wrinkling of nostrils or scowl like a gorgon.
Wherever we go, to the left and the right,
There are beams unaffected and simple delight.

The canopy opening is rapid and clever,
The wind on my cheek a benevolent zephyr.
It gusts round the cockpit, it riffles my hair,
And it whips up some documents high in the air.

Oh my word! It's the essays! They've gone in the breeze!
They blind a meat-pie van, they paper the trees.
Up snatched by the wind-gods they flutter and soar
And blizzard the side of the A404.

Whatever is nitpicking, anal and legal
Is borne to the Chilterns as if by an eagle.
Yes, pigeons will line the connubial bed
With essays coherent but only half-read,

And oversexed mammals will stealthily come
And pillage the papers for use in the home.
And good! Since whatever a Morgan is for
It's hardly the place for an essay on law.

Now the leathery bucket is empty and bare
So I offer the seat to a girl with dark hair,
And the engine returns to its anapaest hum:
Titty tum titty tum titty tum titty tum.

Vital statistics

Built at the family-owned and run Malvern Link factory, the Aero 8 is the world's first all aluminium coach-built car.

Engine BMW 4.4-litre, V8, 286bhp at 5400rpm
Performance 0–60mph in 4.5 secs, top speed 160mph
Price (2003) £53,191: leather interior £2,000 extra

EMISSION STATEMENT

Toyota's fume-cutting Prius is a breath of fresh air.

The M1, somewhere near Luton, a boiling Saturday. The air con had conked in the vast petrol-powered Toyota zeppelin which is the normal Johnson motor. One child was eating crisps, crunch, crunch, crunch, in my ear. Another child was expressing a desire to vomit, breaking off occasionally to wallop another child, who was sobbing. A fourth was insisting that we turn up Madonna, the better to hear the lyrics.

'"Die another day"?' I asked myself. 'Why wait? Why not now?' Hieronymus Bosch could not have painted a more harrowing portrait of hell. It wasn't just that I was captain of a cricket team and on the verge of being late. Nor was it the mere fact of the traffic jam: the endless vista of overheating bonnets, crawling like wounded beetles in the sun. As I looked at the haze of petrol fumes, I felt a sense of apocalyptic horror. Suddenly, I knew what it must feel like to be the possessor of a green conscience.

My car, his car, their cars: throbbing, panting, trapped like the Iraqi army retreating down the road to Basra – think of the emissions! Think of the gaseous vapours being given off by my car alone: the shuddering farts of CO_2, more noxious than the weekly discharge of a herd of bean-fed steers. 'If only,' I thought, 'this clapped-out old boiler of a Toyota had been, instead, a Toyota Prius.' What is a Toyota Prius? It is an idea so wonderful, and yet so simple, that it seems incredible that no one thought of it earlier.

After more than a century, Toyota has come up with the first major improvement on the internal combustion engine. It is a gizmo which allows the car to be run either independently or indeed simultaneously with the petrol engine, by a nickel-metal battery. And this battery is repeatedly recharged – this is the really clever bit – whenever the petrol motor is running. So if you are idling, or inching forward with

The Toyoto Prius features the Toyota Hybrid System that incorporates a petrol engine with an electric zero-emissions motor.

agonising slowness on the M1, when the sweat is trickling off your nose and the children are trying to stick Peperamis into your ear, the petrol motor simply switches off.

The engine goes silent. Your emissions fall to zero. At that moment, the exhaust coming out of your tailpipe is as sweet and harmless as a baby's breath. Not only are you saving petrol – since the Prius can achieve an amazing 52mpg in the cities – you are also doing your bit to save the planet, since it produces 90 per cent less CO_2 emissions than other family saloons of comparable size. And yet still, in the words of Galileo, it moves.

Without consuming a drop of hydrocarbon, without a single detonation in the cylinders, your Prius moves forward, because it is running on battery; and so it will continue – until you need some oomph. It is only as you start moving up through the gears, and flooring the throttle, that the petrol engine comes on again. The beauty of this car is that it is a hybrid. It's the car that thinks it's a milk float but also a Maserati. It is an ingenious piece of evolution, the mechanical equivalent of the female goby fish that lie around waiting for a male goby, and then think, 'Oh what the hell!' and turn into a male goby for 24 hours out of sheer biological necessity. It is the first car to adapt to the misery this Government has inflicted on road users, not just in jacking up the price of petrol, but also in lengthening journey times and the general traffic hell. The wonder, as I said, is that no one has thought of it sooner. If you want to understand the miracle, take out your mobile phone. When I was first issued with a mobile telephone, it was a pretty substantial item; almost as big as a .44 Magnum. The next one was smaller, though with no loss of battery power. I managed to destroy both. Now, after eight years of mobile technology development, I have a phone so absurdly small and girlish it could have come from a Christmas cracker.

It's about the size and weight of a Pringles crisp, and the other day it occurred to me that if the police ever pulled me over for using it while driving I could just swallow the evidence. But the really interesting feature of this new mobile is that it seems to have as much battery power as the first – if not more. And that, pretty much, is the secret of the Prius. In the old days, you would have needed a Portakabin-sized battery to drive the transmission of a car. But

Toyota has been making them smaller and smaller; and the one in the latest Prius is 60 per cent smaller and 30 per cent lighter than the 1997 version.

It's the car that thinks it's a milk float but also a Maserati. It is an ingenious piece of evolution.

In fact, the battery seems to be a matter of deep commercial secrecy. If you open the bonnet, you will find a sign on the battery cover telling you that this is the intellectual property of Toyota, and that no one but a Toyota technician is allowed to look inside. Cor! I am not sure whether the technicians at Honda feel obliged to obey these instructions, but it is still something to be driving a car with a motor so revolutionary that the punter is not allowed to know how it works.

All I can say is that it does work. The Prius gives you a comfortable drive, with plenty of footroom, headroom, armroom and all the rest of it. It moves at a very respectable clip, has all mod cons and all the while you can look at the VDU, which shows you the pathetic quantities of petrol you are using, and how generally eco-friendly you are. The Prius is as clean as Snow White, and as green as grass. It makes you feel good to use it, and we all need to feel good about ourselves sometimes.

Vital statistics

In Latin, 'prius' means 'to go before', a fitting name for a car ahead of its time.

Engine
Petrol engine: 1.5litre, 71bhp at 4,500rpm. Electric motor: 44bhp at 1,040rpm
Performance 0–62mph in 13.4 secs, top speed 99mph
Price (2003) £16,405

PORSCHE POWER

The 911 stands for all that is good.

Apparently, the funsters on *Have I Got News For You*, the hilarious TV gameshow, mentioned my name the other day and everyone groaned. I didn't see it myself, since I was making a vital speech about fluoridation of water, but my sources say it went like this. 'That Boris Johnson,' said Paul Merton, the merriest jester that ever wore motley, 'he turned up at a meeting of Tory MPs, and guess what kind of car he was driving?'

To which Ian Hislop, the frolicsome giggle-king, said, 'I don't know! Tell us what kind of car he was driving.' 'He was driving a Porsche,' said Merton, waving his bladder triumphantly, to signal the birth of the joke. And at that point, I am sad to say, the audience groaned.

Ever since, in my super-sensitive way, I have been trying to work out what provoked their disgust. It was, I am told, a particularly despairing efflatus, a breathy downwards glissando, like the school organ preparing for the last verse of 'Abide With Me'. Was the car the cause of this groan? Or was it (gulp) me?

Let me say immediately that it cannot

have been the car, or not the car alone. What a *Krautwagen*! I want to pay tribute to everyone at *GQ* responsible for securing me the temporary use of this vehicle. Recently, I have tended to be given people carriers to test, and since these are not so much sports cars as mobile invitations to vasectomy, it was cheering to be offered something as nakedly macho as the 911 Targa. But my principal tribute is of course to the makers of the car itself.

I salute not just their brilliance in creating an awesome engine, capable of taking you

The Porsche 911 Targa – where the premium convertible meets the high-performance coupé.

in very short order to a top speed of 177mph. I admire not only their skill in creating a huge retractable roof, thought to be the largest piece of mobile glass ever used on top of a Porsche, comparable to a whale's foreskin in size and retractability. Above all I admire the bravery of the johnnies at Porsche.

Yes, bravery. Just think of the name, and its implications, and I don't mean the Targa bit. It cannot be long before Targa appears, along with Posh and Charlotte, among the ten most popular names of girls whose births are announced in the pages of *The Times*.

The problem is the 911 bit. That's right! Two years after 11 September 2001, the Germans are selling a car overtly named after 9/11, the most infamous terrorist attack in history. You might as well market the Nissan Osama or, indeed, the Datsun Pearl Harbor. How the hell do the boys at Porsche expect a patriotic US yuppie to react? There must be some consumers there who are wondering whether this is a deliberate provocation.

And it is, alas, true that there is anti-Americanism in modern Germany, just as there is in France, and Britain, come to that. But I refuse to believe that this name is in any way intended to be an insult to the USA, for two reasons. The first is that Porsche would not intentionally inflict such a commercial injury upon itself. The second, obviously, is that the name 'nine eleven' comfortably pre-dates 9/11.

History does not record exactly when it was that Heinrich Frankfurter, student of Ferdinand Porsche, devised the all-steel monocoque, hot-galvanised on all sides, which gives these cars their distinctive shape and beauty. Legend has it that a British journalist, lost in admiration, said: 'I'm just checking – are there 12 letters in your surname, Mr Frankfurter?' To which he replied, '*Nein!* Eleven!'

This name, in other words, is a reminder of abiding German values of craftsmanship and industrial innovation. Far from being provocative to keep the name after the attacks of 11 September, it would have been pathetic not to keep it. To jettison one of Porsche's most famous brands because it sounds like the anniversary of a terrorist outrage would be doing bin Laden's work for him. It would have been a capitulation to terror.

That is why it is such a pleasure to buy coffee from the Manhattan Coffee Shop, in a cup which is still decorated with the Two Towers, proud, unforgotten, giving two fingers to Islamic maniacs across London.

I was proud to drive the Targa, it's gorgeous. I urge you to go out and get one.

That is why, as a Conservative and a conservative, and a supporter of the USA, I was proud to drive a Porsche 911 Targa to the Tory bonding session.

As for the groaning of the audience on *Have I Got News For You*, I have only one explanation. They did not object to the Porsche. How could they? It is a gorgeous machine and I urge you to get one immediately. I don't think they were even actuated by resentment of me. Their feeling was pure jealousy, and how can you blame them? Merton gave them the clear impression that I owned the car, when in fact I was only borrowing it for a weekend – a blatant and unashamed attempt to arouse feelings of envy in the breasts of the British public, and to direct those feelings against a Tory MP. And it was based on a lie! But what else can you expect from the BBC?

Vital statistics

The glass roof of the Porsche 911 retracts in just 8 secs.

Engine 3.6 litre, 320bhp flat six
Performance 0–62mph in 5.2 secs, top speed 177mph
Price (2003) £61,550

GO FORTH AND MULTIPLY

Chrysler's Voyager is set to trigger a breeding frenzy.

Shall I tell you how you feel, when you bomb down the motorway in the Chrysler Grand Voyager Limited XS? You feel terrific. You feel a bit like a whale, but a sleek, porpoising whale, nosing aside the BMWs and the Ford Focuses as if they were minnows.

You feel a bit like a Zeppelin, whooshing aloft, your eyeline higher than everyone else's. But the main reason you feel terrific is that you feel fertile.

Whatever else the Chrysler Voyager says about you, this car tells the world that you are not firing blanks. You don't need one of those irritating yellow Lib-Dem-type signs saying, 'Baby on board'. The Chrysler Voyager is a mobile advertisement for the fact that you have been repeatedly engaged in the noble business of reproducing the human race.

Many a car is designed to make the driver look sexy. Every year there are dozens of sleek models constructed as if to proclaim that there is a 'Bonker on board'. If you drive the Chrysler Voyager, with its seven seats and 14 (count 'em! 14!) cup holders, the world rather gathers that you have been bonking for Britain. Let us imagine that you bought a Voyager without first acquiring some kids to fill it.

I am not saying that would necessarily be a foolish thing to do. This vehicle has all kinds of attractions for the bachelor of the parish. It goes like the clappers for an object of this size, what with the 3.3-litre engine. It has a cool eight-way adjustable driver's seat, with the armrests like the ones on the chair Hemingway used to fish marlin. It has a state-of-the-art stereo and air con and everything else.

If you drive the Chrysler Voyager, with its seven seats and 14 (count 'em! 14!) cup holders, the world rather gathers that you have been bonking for Britain.

And yet I suggest that there might come a time, as you toddled along on your own, when you felt that you were not exhausting the potential of the machine. There are ten hi-fi speakers dotted around the vast cabin. There are three separate zones for the air con. There is an in-car DVD entertainment system for anyone sitting in the back rows.

You remember in Richmal Crompton's *Just William* books, when William gets a penknife that has one of those special blades for getting the stones out of horses' hooves. He feels a bit depressed about this accessory, and then it hits him that he must get a horse to go with it! That's how you will feel: a couple of days sitting at the wheel of the Voyager, and you'll be yearning to punch out some babies to go with the cup holders.

It is my view, in fact, that Voyagers and MPVs like it are not just a response to the needs of families. They promote that need. They encourage fecundity. Get a family with one or two children into a Voyager, and I guarantee there will come a moment when mummy looks at daddy in a smouldering way, and they decide that they might as well make use of the three seats at the back. In so far as this analysis is correct, these MPVs are playing a vital part in the future of our nation, and I've the statistics to prove it.

You'll be familiar with the catastrophic decline in the fertility of the average British woman from 1964 to 1978. As we all know, our parents were going at it hammer and tongs in the early Sixties, and the tongs were vibrating most vigorously against the hammer in 1964. This was in many ways a vintage year; not only the year in which your motoring correspondent drew his first breath, but also the year of maximum productivity by the average British woman, who was then popping out a stakhanovite three babies.

Then something terrible happened. Maybe it was the pill. Maybe it was feminism. Maybe some foreign power put something in the water supply. Whatever the reason, the fertility rate slumped to about 1.7 babies per woman of childbearing age. And that's not enough to replenish the population, even assuming that people live longer. From that moment, we have been living with a worsening dependency ratio. We have more and more old people, who depend on the taxes generated by the earnings of fewer and fewer young people. Panic!

Some politicians, such as David Willetts, the Shadow Work and Pensions Secretary, have suggested that Britain needs Mussolini-style have-a-baby bounties. But there may be other options that don't involve more public spending.

Look at the fertility chart over the last 50 years, and you will find astonishing evidence that the MPV is an incentive to reproduction. After they slumped to 1.7 babies per mother in

1978, the Brits got bonking again. By 1981, they were up to 1.9 babies per mother; and why? It's obvious, innit? It was about that time, of course, that the first people carrier, the Renault Espace, appeared on the market. By the early Nineties, as the novelty of the Espace was wearing off, the graph begins to slip again. Then, round about 1994, it kicks up. Why? Because of the impact on the British market of this US machine, the Chrysler Voyager.

According to Trevor Creed, Senior Vice President of Design, Chrysler has sold ten million Voyagers since 1983. Now imagine that, in every case, there was a family that decided to expand by two kids to make use of some of the cup holders. That means, at a conservative estimate, that the Voyager has been responsible for the creation of 20 million human beings.

Let us assume that Britain has one twentieth of the market for Voyagers: that means the machine has added a million kids to our stock of human capital. There, my friends, in the gloom of the pensions crisis, is the glimmering of hope. It's the car that thinks it's a maternity ward.

Vital statistics

The Chrysler Grand Voyager is built with safety in mind – there are driver and front passenger airbags, energy-absorbing bumpers, side-impact door beams and halo headrests on all of the seats.

Engine 3.3-litre V6, 172bhp
Performance 0–62mph in 12.6 secs, top speed 111mph
Price (2004) £29,300

THE SLEEPING POLICEMAN'S NEMESIS

Look down on the humps in a Freelander.

Clunk clink chonk. 'Christ on a bike,' I thought, as I scraped the Bic over the chin. 'I know that noise.' It was 8.43am on a freezing Islington morning. Across the benighted borough, swarms of traffic wardens were being disgorged from their big white mother vans. They were being issued with maps of the local parking zones, and beginning their fell work. And to judge by the *rattle clank chunk chonk* that came through my fogged-up bathroom window, they had found my illegally parked Land Rover Freelander and, in the space of only 13 minutes, called in the clampers.

I rubbed a circle in the misty pane. Yup. There was no time to lose. Maybe it was the sight of your Motoring Correspondent wearing nothing but towel. Maybe it was my merry opening cry of, '**** off you ****ing ****ers!' But for once I prevailed on the heartless bastards who enforce the parking regulations round our London house. 'You're just in time,' beamed the clamper, and, *chonk chink clank*, he unlocked his evil device, in what must surely be an act of unprecedented clemency. He would give me five minutes to repark the car legally, he said. So I did, and discovered that one good thing about the Freelander is that it is ideal for driving with no clothes on.

In fact, this is the sort of behaviour, imagine, that is popular with Freelander owners across the world. There you are, lying by some waterhole in the Serengeti, having just finished making love to your girlfriend. You look up, and snakes alive, a gang of Masai are sneaking up on your

One good thing about the Freelander is that it is ideal for driving with no clothes on.

vehicle. So you leap aboard, and the diesel begins its reassuring rumble. You hit the clutch and the car lurches off like a warthog with a trod-on ingrown toenail. The soft leather cushions your quivering buttocks; the air con is like the breeze that blows over the veld round about teatime. And, wham, you wallop that first anthill with the offside front wheel, and soon you are bounding and hummocking over the grass at 40 or 50mph. It is only after you have covered half the Ngorongoro crater that, Cee-ripes, you remember that you've left your naked girlfriend in the care of the assegai-wielding Masai. Oh well, you think, and turn on the CD.

So I made my escape from the traffic wardens of Islington, and as the Freelander galloped in search of a legitimate parking space, I made another discovery. The borough, under its communist Liberal Democrat junta, charges the highest council taxes in the universe. Much of this charge goes on traditional Islington causes: gay and lesbian community coordinators, outreach workers and so on, all no doubt a fine investment in society. But every year the Liberal Democrat tyrants find they have a problem.

They have taxed so much, and gouged so much from the impecunious pensioners, that they run out of obvious ways to squander the loot in time for next year's budget settlement, when they must renew their demands. So they have come up with a brilliant Keynesian solution. They close off the roads with cones and red and white booms, and flashing lights. At the general expense they commission the services of hordes of unintelligible Balkan navvies. And they build humps. With Pharaonic ambition, they build enormous tarmac pillows all over the roads.

They totally wreck the Queen's highway as a place for vehicular traffic, because if you approach these monstrous impediments at more than 20mph you scrape your prow on the way up, and then you scrape your keel on the way down. It is a torture and a disgrace. The other day I was proceeding at the speed of a bath chair, and one of these humps whacked the rear end of my Toyota so hard that the spare tyre fell out, a loss I only discovered when I got home.

So you can imagine that over the last few years I have been trying to think of the answer. Surely, I have reasoned, these bumps represent the kind of challenge to the human spirit that results in technological progress. The sword produced the shield. Stone fortifications inspired the trebuchet. The trenches and barbed wire were finally answered by tanks. And now, ladies and gentlemen, in the cold dawn of 2004, the odious Liberal Democrat road humps have met their match in the Land Rover Freelander.

'Yeehah!' I shouted as I took the first set of sleeping policemen at speed, and the machine hardly quivered. The suspension soaked it up. The clock on the dashboard did not miss a beat. There was scarcely a rattle fore and aft as I took the next humps faster still. In any other vehicle, I can assure you, this would have been madness. The car would have kangarooed so violently that both bumpers would have clanged on to the street, and the exhaust pipe would have been driven like a spear into the heart of the engine.

But in the Freelander? No worries. I scudded over those beastly bumps like a hovercraft, and never again will I denounce those who use 4x4s in town. The paradox is that there is no real call for them in the countryside these days: the place is full of tarmac ribbons. The Freelander may be useful anywhere, but thanks to the Liberal Democrats, and their sadistic traffic policies, the car's natural habitat is Islington.

Vital statistics

Pretenders to the throne come and go but the 'baby Land Rover' remains Europe's best-selling 4x4 and the 2004 version has been redesigned inside and out.

Engine: 2 litre, 4-cylinder, turbo diesel
Performance: 0–60mph in 13.2 secs, top speed 100mph
Price: (2004) £22,600

MIND CONTROL

The Lotus Elise 111S: a redline experience to scramble your grey matter.

This was bad. This was as bad as it gets. I have had car cock-ups before. But in an exceedingly tightly congested field, this was the biggest car cock-up of all time.

I think sometimes in my expert evaluations of these cars, with my assessments of torque and what have you, I fail to convey a full sense of the logistical difficulties involved in doing this job. The car turns up on Friday. It is parked in my street in Islington. In the first five minutes it gets a ticket. It is then clamped. Then towed away.

Over the years I have received wonderfully tense letters from Condé Nast, which owns *GQ*, about these matters. Condé Nast's financial officers take a dim view of my parking tickets and at one stage docked my pay. 'It is not company policy to assist its contributors in springing cars from car pounds,' they said. And I want Condé Nast to know that I agree, in all sincerity. But today I was in a serious fix. Not only had the car been towed, I couldn't remember what it looked like, or what colour it was.

We had been to the Regis Road car

pound in Kentish Town. We had been to the Old Street car park in Camden. My secretary, Ann, tried to discover the truth. 'Come on now,' she said in her honeyed Batley, West Yorkshire tones, waving her sjambok and standing over me. 'Was it green or purple?' 'I think it was kind of greeny-purply-blue,' I said. And the abortive search went on.

The new version of the Lotus Elise 111S maintains the performance of a racing car, but with essential creature comforts.

'Oh Lord,' I thought. I took some Nurofen, lay down, shut my eyes, and tried to think myself back into the tiny Lotus Elise 111S, which I had been driving only the previous Friday evening, and driving it, I may say, like the clappers. I seemed to think the car was wedge-shaped, with wavy bits above the wheels, like the flaring nostrils of a pin-goaded stallion. It was small, not much bigger than a dining room table. In fact, when I first jemmied myself inside the thing, and looked at its ever so slightly placcy accoutrements, I don't remember being impressed. It was a bit rattly, and it was virtually impossible to hear the radio, and you could hardly see out of the back at all.

I couldn't remember what it looked like, or what colour it was.

'What,' I asked myself, 'do people see in these Lotus jobbies? Why is this still a marque of style and distinction?' And of course these heretical thoughts occurred on the way out to Wiltshire on the M4 on Friday evening – as good a definition of hell on earth as I have yet come across. I got so depressed in the traffic that I could hardly bear to press down on the throttle, even when the traffic cleared, and was consequently overtaken by all manner of Datsun Sunnys and bath chairs. It was, however, a different story on the way back.

As usual, I had given a torrential speech to a huge gathering of Tories, dwelling, *inter alia*, on this government's persecution of the motorist. I seem to think it may be that my memory is playing me false that they gave me a standing ovation. At any rate it was in a moderately superb frame of mind that I shoehorned myself back into the Lotus, like a magician getting a hard-boiled egg into a bottle, and allowed it to convey me back to London. I put it that way, because the journey seemed to involve so little volition on my part. That car may be small, but it is the performing flea of the motoring world. It is the mouse that roared.

We flew back down that motorway so fast that as Wiltshire dissolved into Berkshire, and then Acton, as the 1.8-litre engine packed a punch of cars double the horsepower and three times the price, I must have gone into a trance. And there, my friends, is the explanation for my amnesia.

'Look,' I said to Ann, once she had finished flagellating me with rolled-up copies of *Horse and Hound*, 'I know why I can't remember the colour of the car. It was just going too fast. It was red shift. It was the Doppler effect. It was one of those special colours that are known only to linguistic philosophers. It was grue. It was bleen. It was emerire. It was sapphald.'

'Oh aye,' said the Batley girl, whacking me again, 'well you go to the pound and identify it, then.' There was nothing for it. I did. We found that beautiful Lotus, which turned out to be green. Or possibly purple. Yup. It's the Lotus, the car that's so damn fast you can't even tell the colour. That's my story and I'm sticking to it.

Vital statistics

Engine 1.8-litre VVC, 143bhp
Performance 0–62mph in 5.38 secs, top speed 133mph
Price (2004) £27,995

NOBLE SAVAGE

To impress the kids, Boris took them out in the Noble M12 GTO-3R – the daddy of all supercars.

One of the things about these nine-year-olds is that they become progressively more difficult to impress. Children begin by thinking you are a combination of Alan Shearer and James Bond. But you take them out to the park to show your football skills, and after a while the blighters are contemptuously nutmegging you, so that you slip on a wet patch and bruise your coccyx.

To all fathers, therefore, who may be feeling that they wished they could once again provoke that first shining-eyed fervour of filial admiration, this is the solution.

It's called the Noble M12 GTO-3R, and when I came in one afternoon, and casually told the heirs to the Johnson millions that it was pinking outside, I was amazed by the reaction. 'Did you say a Noble?' asked the nine-year-old. He couldn't believe that the *GQ* car department had entrusted such a supercar to a clapped-out old trout like me.

'But how do you know about it?' I asked him. 'It's in Top Trumps, innit?' he said.

Top Trumps? 'Ah!' I said, 'Top Trumps! Now there was a game.' The winners, I said,

Vital statistics

Noble no longer sells its cars via dealers – but buying direct means that prices are cheaper.

Engine: 3-litre V6, 352bhp
Performance: 0–60mph in 3.7 secs, top speed 170mph
Price: (2004) £49,950

the cars you needed for speed, were the Jaguar E-type and the Jensen Interceptor III.

Jaguars? Jensens? said my boy. Didn't I realise that I had a machine outside that could knock them into a cocked hat? Listen, Pop, he said, or words to this effect, the car you have outside has a Ford 3-litre V6 Duratec engine, and it has been engineered to deliver 360 brake horsepower. This is in the elite category of British supercars! Why don't we see what it can do?

To all fathers wishing to once again provoke that first shining-eyed fervour of filial admiration, this is the solution.

'OK, kiddo,' I said. And we went for a spin. But this being London traffic, we went slower than a Waitrose trolley being pushed by a peg-legged grandmother. Only by flooring it away from the traffic lights were we able to discern any hint of the machine's potential. In those few seconds, however, I saw a look in the kid's eyes and the light of the old acclaim. 'Cor!' he said. 'Was that you doing it, or was it the car?'

'I don't know,' I said, and I didn't. But when I took the car for a proper drive, up and down the M40 to Oxfordshire, I was aware that something big might happen – that it might achieve a speed truly unassailable in Top Trumps. And it did. I felt

as though I had driven a proper car;
something of steel and aluminium and
featherlight handling and indescribable
pace. I felt nine years old. So I want to
thank Lee Noble for the ride, and to

congratulate him on building a machine for all the Johnson family. 'Can we buy it?' the nine-year-old asked when I brought it in to land for the second time. 'I don't know,' I said. 'Can we?'

The speedy Noble M12 GTO-3R is in a class all of its own.

CONTINENTAL DIVIDE

When it comes to class, there's Bentley and then all the rest.

Now say the word Bentley to yourself and see what flashes up in your mind. I bet you think of a certain type of machine. You see a vast sea swell of dove-grey metal. You see a footman skipping to the door. You see two lizard skin-clad feet emerging, chinchilla body, a tight little black hat pinned with platinum and diamonds, a face belonging to some supermodel marchioness and a voice issuing a command such as, 'Thank you, Lawson, and could you bring it round to the front of the hotel at four?'

That is what the word Bentley connotes, isn't it? When a man arrives in a Bentley, it is a sign that he has *really* arrived. And when nemesis comes, and a great commercial empire collapses, there is normally a Bentley there somewhere, so huge, so expensive, that the City wouldn't put up with it any more.

One thinks of the Bentley as the refuge of some intercontinental tycoon, hounded by rebellious shareholders, betrayed by his own hand-picked board, speeding in tint-windowed silence in his leveraged limousine, desperately trying to raise a loan from the traitors of New York, and taking what last comfort he can in the softness and luxury and space of the kid-leather cabin. The Lear jet has been sold; Malibu has been repossessed; but the car is still enormous, and that is the point of it.

I remember the Bentleys at the school sports day, ranged on the cricket pitches like dreadnoughts at Spithead, churning the grass to a fine mud; and I remember the surprising number of giggling young girls who would issue from each car and fan out over the lawns in pursuit of acnoid young men. So when Paul Henderson, *GQ* car supremo, said that I was going to have a Bentley for the weekend, I was looking forward to a four-wheeled superfortress of steel and comfort; and that is why I was curious to see what turned up.

This particular Bentley was certainly butch. It was bulky.

'Eeyup, our Boris,' said Ann Sindall, my assistant, a forthright Yorkshirewoman from the town of Batley. 'Eeyup,' she said, 'how are you going to fit the kids in that?' The truth about this particular Bentley, the Continental GT, is that it was certainly butch. It was bulky. It sat kind of hunched on its forequarters like some muscular grey panther or snow leopard. But it was not enormous. It frankly did not possess the kind of sweeping supertanker prow one associates with a machine normally hired by blubbering fathers to take their daughters away, once the marriage ceremony has been performed, to face the terrors of their wedding night.

And that was very much the point made to me by John Redwood MP, when I turned up in my Bentley that afternoon at the Tory 'bonding' weekend. I should explain that a Tory 'bonding' weekend is a conference at a hotel in Hertfordshire, where Tory MPs come together to share the joys and pains of being Tory MPs. I had a feeling that the

Bentley – yours for £112,750 – was not perhaps the ideal adhesive for a bonding weekend, and so it proved.

John Redwood is a prize fellow of All Souls. He can be a man of uncommon brilliance and charm. But when he looked at my Bentley, I was reminded of the way he used to look at single mothers on council estates in Wales when he was Welsh Secretary in John Major's cabinet. 'Hmmm,' he said, 'I don't see why I should pay all that money for a glorified BMW.' I was still smarting at this insult to the essential Britishness of the car when Redders went on, still more woundingly, 'And anyway, the bonnet is too short.'

I had a feeling that the Bentley – yours for £112,750 – was not perhaps the ideal adhesive for a Tory bonding weekend, and so it proved.

I looked again at the bonnet, and I remembered that John is an E-type Jaguar man. He drives a car with perhaps the longest bonnet that has ever been offered to the motoring public. I cannot now speculate on the psychological reasons that impel John or anyone else to drive a car with such a long bonnet; all I can say is that I looked at my own Bentley bonnet and felt vaguely embarrassed. Was it really too short? Was there something wrong with it?

Was I in some sense inadequate to be driving a car with such a short bonnet?

There was nothing for it. That weekend I drove the entire family to Sussex and Oxfordshire in that Bentley, and I want you to know that it was of Tardis-like capaciousness within. This is a wonderful, wonderful car, with the best sat-nav system I have ever used, all the acceleration you need to get in and out of trouble, a seriously lusty six-litre engine, and enough room, in spite of its coupé looks, to take four children very long distances with no ill-effects whatsoever (except when one of them decided to work out what the cigarette lighter was).

Thank you, Paul and everyone else at *GQ*, for letting me have a Bentley Continental GT for the weekend. I think my good friend John Redwood is quite wrong about its merits. As for the length of the bonnet, I don't know what my wife thought of it but if she did have any reservations she was kind enough not to complain.

Vital statistics

This is the first Bentley to be produced by VW since it bought the famous old brand in 1998.

Engine 6-litre, 12-cylinder, 552bhp twin turbochargers
Performance 0–60mph in 4.7 secs, top speed 198mph
Price (2004) £112,750

WEIRD SCIENCE

Artificial intelligence and alpha-male styling: the new Mercedes SLK could be the car of the future.

It happens to Hal in *2001: A Space Odyssey*. It happens in the *Terminator* films. It happens in *I, Robot*. It appears to be a standard plot device in just about every sci-fi film. Somehow I can't believe it's happening to us now, but it is: the on-board computer has gone nuts.

The automatic pilot has had a fit of electronic epilepsy. It can no longer distinguish between its cybernetic arse and its android elbow. 'Proceed north up the M1,' says the computer voice. It is a measure of the natural authority vested in this beautiful German-built machine, and its Einstein sat-nav, that at first I don't question the order.

We proceed north. We proceed at speed. We whoosh through the sodium night like a blue dart, the prow cleaving the air with its snarling wedge designed like some Einsteinian anomaly of the space-time continuum to be both retro and futuristic.

We proceed so fast that when I look at

the handsome map of the sat-nav, I can see us surging north in a blue line, like the lightning advance of Heinz Guderian's Panzers across the Polish lowlands. It is only when we see the first sign for Luton that I start to wonder. Normally I would not dream of pitting my brain – a few pounds of wine-pickled offal – against the silicon genius. But it suddenly hits me that this is the road to Scotland, and that my house is in London.

It may take you to Aberdeen, but the SLK's sat-nav system sure looks good.

Unless this SLK is so fast that it is proposing to circumnavigate the planet, we are travelling in precisely the wrong direction. In order to reach my house before breakfast, we must now perform a 180-degree turn, and surely the computer knows this. Surely it can remember that I tapped in an address in Islington, London, not Aberdeen.

And yet, such is my admiration for this machine that as the junction approaches it requires a huge effort of will to override its commands. 'Continue on the M1,' advises the sat-nav, and the sweat pops on my brow, like Captain Kirk struggling to snap out of some extraterrestrial hypnosis.

'No, no, no,' I shriek, at least inwardly. 'You've gone mad, you crazy car-brain. My home and bed is back there, getting more distant every second.'

'Follow the road ahead,' says the car, with what sounds to my ears like a hint of menace.

At last, with a spastic lunge, I turn the wheel left, off the motorway, and find the southbound carriageway. I am slightly trembly, as one just sprung from a cult.

Without so much as an apologetic cough, the sat-nav then drives me home by precisely contradicting its earlier instructions, showing that it would have a great career at the top of British politics. 'Why,' I ponder to myself as I drive, 'did this peerless machine make this elementary goof?' The simplest answer is that it was an electronic malfunction; but I find that hard to believe. Not an SLK. Not a car as slick as this.

I prefer to think that the car knew exactly what it was doing, and it was trying to show who was boss. To understand the psychology of the SLK, you have to go back eight years, to that glorious moment when I began my career as a motoring correspondent. I reviewed the first Mercedes SLK for the *Daily Telegraph*, and recorded my sensations of pleasure at taking my wife to the Newbury races. I wrote rapturously about the handling, the 57 sexy little motors that make the roof go up and down in less time than it takes the lights to change on the Marylebone Road. It was a piece of such exuberance that I am proud to say it caught the eye of the editor of *GQ*, who engaged my services.

Other reviewers, I was amazed to discover, were less warm-hearted. One man, shockingly, described the original SLK

Vital statistics

The Mercedes SLK 200 Kompressor comes with a system called Airscarf that blows hot air on to your neck as you drive for extra top-down comfort.

Engine 1.8-litre, 163bhp
Performance 0–62mph in 7.9 secs, top speed 143mph
Price (2005) £27,540

Kompressor as a 'girlie' car. Girlie! A car as fast as this! I would have said that the original SLK was as zappy and red-blooded as the next car, diminutive though it was. It was a gross insult, and yet it plainly stung.

For the past eight years the SLK team has been brooding on this insult to their machine's virility. The new model is plainly designed to be a retort, an assertion of machismo; and unless we fail to get the point, the Stuttgart copywriter has written an 80-page hymn to the maleness of this machine which I recommend that you read aloud to yourself in a screamingly camp German accent.

The Mercedes SLK is a great car. But it's not the kind of car that likes to admit it's wrong.

'The 16-inch wheels underline the muscular nature of the new SLK class. Widely flared wings extend around the well-filled wheel arches like perfectly toned muscles, symbolising the athletic power of the roadster. The body-language is clear: in these areas the metal skin is intentionally tailored to be rather tight and "body-conscious", with pronounced curves that arouse curiosity about the muscles concealed beneath.'

Muscles! *Jawohl!* On and on he goes, about the 'muscular contour of the wing and the prominent curvature of the bonnet'.

Most car manufacturers would be content to say that their car had a boot and a rear bumper, but that would not do justice to the virility of the new SLK. According to the bard of Stuttgart there is a 'flowing cord of muscle' around the rump of the car, 'a powerfully accentuated rear apron'.

After writing all this drooling car porn, one imagines that he went out to some disco wearing a tank top and lederhosen and was obligingly murdered by a rent boy with a powerfully accentuated rear apron.

But he is right. It is a great car. And it is also a proud car. It's not the kind of car that likes to admit it is wrong, and there, perhaps, we have the explanation for its curious decision to take me to London from Hampshire by way of Aberdeen.

It is a widely remarked upon distinction between the male and female minds, that the woman will often admit that she is lost, while the man will blast on forever up the wrong road. There you have the spirit of the new SLK, even more manly than the old one. If that were possible.

YOU CAN WITH THIS NISSAN

Boris Johnson gives the paparazzi a run for their money in the lively 350Z.

10.30am. It's a dull, cold morning and it is also – though I don't know it yet – the day on which I will experience what we politicians call 'a little local difficulty'. I have no idea, as I step out on to the Camden street, that the clock is ticking and that in only a few hours I will cease to glory in my role as Shadow Minister for the Arts.

But I know that my enemies are starting to close in on me, and my hungover eyes scope out the terrain. He's there. Of course he is.

The *News of the World* snapper is waiting for me in his hilarious, tint-windowed, mod-conned Land Rover, with bull bars and about 12 headlights, some of them mounted as if for lamping rabbits, and – doubtless – a rabbit is how he thinks I feel. But no. Not today. Not I. I am not going to give in easily, because at this critical juncture in my life story I have been given a Nissan to drive: a 350Z, the most exhilaratingly sporty Nissan ever made.

As I unlock it, I see the reporter do a double take and then scamper back to his Land Rover. He can't believe it's my car.

'Tee hee,' I say, and start the engine, not any old engine but the awesome 3.5-litre V6, hailed by *Ward's Auto World* – every year for the last 11 years – as one of the world's ten best. Arum, goes the engine, arum arum arum araaaah, and the car snouts from the parking spot like a questing panther. 'Right, you tabloid buggers,' I think, 'I'm going to give you the slip.'

10.35am. Alas, I forget that I am in a one-way street, and by the time I sort it out, I find the cocky little bastard is on my tail.

10.35.00001am. Turn into Mornington Crescent and put the machine through warp-factor six.

10.35.00002am. *Teufel!* The Land Rover is still on my tail, and in traffic like this there's nothing much to be done about it.

I howl out of my parking place in a pall of rubber and lean back my head in a rich, easy laugh of triumph.

10.59am. I pick up a companion from Notting Hill and explain the problem. She looks at the snapper, who has parked up on a double yellow next to her house. We can see him through the tint windows. He is cheerfully blazing away, and then down comes the window and out comes a telephoto lens the size of a milk churn.

The camera mews like an impudent seagull. I want to punch his lights out. I walk towards the Land Rover, grimacing strangely.

'I'm really sorry,' says the snapper, lowering his camera. 'They told me to follow you all day. I am only doing my job,' he says.

'Oh all right,' I say. I still want to punch his lights out, but I am overcome by a sudden and ignoble feeling of solidarity with a fellow newspaperman despatched by his desk – as all of us sometimes are – to cover some godawful story. And anyway, I have a better idea.

'Come on,' I say to my companion, 'let's

shake him off.' I select first gear. I rev up. I note that the engine can achieve a peak torque figure of 363Nm at 4,800rpm.

At the very moment when the traffic lights on the corner of Elgin Crescent and Ladbroke Grove are turning from amber to red I howl out of my parking place in a pall of rubber, turn left through the lights, and lean back my head in a rich, easy laugh of triumph.

11.00am. Hell and damnation. He's still there! This is turning into a struggle between two of the greatest commercial empires of the 21st century – Nissan and News International.

I can't believe the adhesive quality of this Murdoch-owned Land Rover. But my Nissan can do 0–62mph in just 5.9 seconds, and here in Notting Hill, I have an advantage. I grew up here, from age 15 to 18. I know the roads. Or at least I think I do. 'Hold on,' I say to my companion and she gives a yelp as we lurch left …

11.01am … down Arundel Gardens, cocooned by the multi-link suspension's amniotic fluid effect …

11.01.34am … and yeeeow, we careen into Kensington Park Road …

11.01.35am … and into Colville Terrace …

11.01.36am … and the wrong way down Portobello Road, scattering American Hugh Grant fans like pigeons …

11.02am … and I can't believe it. I come shooting in triumph out on to Ladbroke Grove again, having done a kind of cat's cradle of the neighbourhood.

And the *News of the World* Land Rover is just waiting for me, and we can almost see his grin through the shaded window. What has he got? Transponders? Homing devices?

12.30pm. But when we get to the motorway the contest with the Land Rover ends decisively in my favour. So it damn well ought to, what with my being at the wheel of a 155mph sports car, and him driving a machine designed for towing cows out of bogs. He manages to keep me in view through the Hammersmith traffic, but when we are on the M4 … good night, baby and amen …

1pm. In fact, I am so enjoying the speed and prowess of the Nissan that I stop really looking in the rear-view mirror. It is only when we reach the turning for ***** that I vaguely notice that there is an Audi Quattro behind us, and that he seems to be going to much the same place.

'Oh boy,' I think. I slow down. The Audi slows down. Yup – I should have realised that the paparazzi wouldn't rely on a Land Rover, not on a motorway. I park in the lovely town of ***** and go up to the Quattro, who parks up on the kerb. He rolls down the window, I know what he is going to say. 'I am only doing my job, Boris,' he whimpers.

3pm to 6pm. And so it goes on, all afternoon. At one stage, while I try to shake off the beastly Quattro down some muddy lane (another dead end, more embarrassed reversing), the posse swells. Another paparazzo turns up, in a clapped-out Toyota Corolla. I am afraid at this stage I give up, and we go back to London in a kind of OJ Simpson convoy down the motorway, the fugitive Nissan pursued by a fleet of photographers.

And in the course of those few hours it would be fair to say that matters evolve, in the phrase of Emperor Hirohito, not necessarily to my political advantage.

But at least I have driven a fabulous 350Z, and shaken off at least one of my pursuers, and if the boys at Nissan are disappointed by my evasive capabilities, let me point out that I had much on my mind, and it took three of them to pin me down.

Vital statistics

The 350Z is the fifth incarnation of the classic Japanese Z-car that was first unveiled more than 35 years ago.

Engine 3.5-litre, V6
Performance 0–62mph in 5.9 secs, top speed 155mph
Price (2005) £24,500

ACCELERATED LEARNING

Boris gets up to speed with the latest Lancer.

I am afraid to say that when the *GQ* team delivered this little number to my London address, the heart failed to quicken in the way that it normally does. 'What the hell,' I thought, as I stared out of the bathroom window, 'is that? Call yourself a sports car?' I muttered as I walked around it.

OK, it had the giant disc brakes, normally evidence of high performance. And it had a wacky tin spoiler on its rear, a flared hydroplane arrangement. But the aerodynamic aid seemed incongruous, frankly, on a car that had all the menace and urgency of a 1987 Morris Maestro.

It was small. It was grey. It was inoffensive, and I like my *GQ* cars to have an element of vulgarity about them, something to cause all my lefty neighbours in Islington to groan. So I left it there all day and went to work by bike, and in the evening it was only with difficulty that I persuaded my wife to get inside it and come out to dinner.

It is a sad fact that my wife and I do not see eye to eye in the matter of cars. I love my *GQ* cars. I am hugely indebted to the editor of *GQ* for allowing me to share my expertise with his readers. But my wife for some reason thinks, and I quote, 'They are all the same and they smell of plastic.' And so when I held open the door of the Mitsubishi Lancer, and invited her and my sister-in-law to get inside, her reaction was predictable.

'Do we have to go in this thing?' she said, arching away. 'It smells of plastic.' 'Oh, come on,' I said, less confident than normal. 'It's a fantastic car, and they say it has got fantastic acceleration.'

I admit that when I said this I had not the foggiest idea about the acceleration of the Lancer, and so I was pleased when I let out the clutch and found the thing bounded away as though an enraged divinity had kicked it in the rear.

To say that it sounded like cavalry charging over a tin bridge would not begin to do justice to the noise of the engine.

'Hey!' said my wife and her sister, bouncing around in the back, 'do you have to drive like that?'

'So-rree!' I said, and we scorched down Liverpool Road towards the posh eatery we had chosen, and I began to see why the car must be the No. 1 choice for the boy racers of today.

To say that it sounded like cavalry

charging over a tin bridge would not begin to do justice to the noise of the engine. Yes, there was cavalry-and-tin-bridge in the mix, just as a wine lover might say there was a hint of raspberry in a vintage bouquet. But there were so many other fine aural flavours in the brew.

There was a suggestion of cement mixer, bubbling porridge and a touch of the school organ shuddering with emotion when all the stops come out for the climax of 'Jerusalem'.

Never mind the dull exterior; the exuberant vulgarity is all in the engine, and it has a lot of oomph.

'For heaven's sake!' shouted the Wheeler sisters, as we roared through Islington, and the blinds snapped up around us and lights went on and annoyed media lefties stuck their turtle heads out – too late – to shout abuse at our departing rear. 'Does it have to make so much noise?' they asked.

'Oh yes,' I said knowledgeably, 'it's built that way. It's good for it to make that noise. It *needs* to make all that noise.' And by the time we had finished dinner and I was driving them home, you will not be surprised to learn that I was becoming very fond of this Lancer.

Never mind the dull exterior; the exuberant vulgarity is all in the engine, and it has a lot of oomph. It accelerates so fast that the rev counter actually waggles, like a reed in the wind, and best of all, for a machine this talented, is that it has a fuzzbuster.

Yes, for the first time in my life I have driven with the gizmo that is now indispensable to every civilised motor. As I have reported before, I am on the verge of being banned from driving. If I am caught speeding one more time, I will be prevented, by the apparatus of the state, from using the Queen's highways; and for the wretches in the same position as me, this Mitsubishi is the answer.

'Dit-dit-dit-dit deeet DEEET,' it goes, as soon as you approach one of the evil money-grubbing Gatsos. 'DEEET,' it says, if you fail to slow down. It is quite amazingly clever, in that the fuzzbuster knows not only where all the speed cameras are, but what speed you are meant to be driving at – and, as anyone who has been clocked on the A40 will know, that is the key question.

I took it to Oxford the following day, and I was able to drive the route fast-ish, safely, and with complete confidence. By the end, it had won my heart. It may be a mousy car to look at, but the Mitsubishi Lancer is the mouse that roared.

I salute Mitsubishi for so brilliantly concealing its potential in this salaryman exterior, and as for the fuzzbuster, it is in the words of that old ad, 'a major contribution to road safety'.

Soon, there will be (I hope) a Tory government, and among our sensible policies is to increase the national speed limit to 80. Until that happy moment, this is the next best thing.

Vital statistics

The Evo VIII FQ400 is Mitsubishi's fastest-ever road car, introduced to mark the 30th anniversary of the company's arrival in the UK.

Engine 2-litre turbo, 405bhp
Performance 0–60mph in 3.5 secs, top speed over 175mph
Price (2005) £46,999

MIND OVER MOTOR

Boris gets a conscience over the Nissan Murano.

Vital statistics

The Murano's 'Birdview' sat-nav also tracks gridlocks via radio and then shows its jam-bypass routes in impressive 3D.

Engine V6, 3,498cc
Performance 0–62mph in 8.9 secs, top speed 124mph
Price (2005) £29,800

In the course of a chequered career as your motoring correspondent. I like to think I have picked up the odd fan. There is, alas, one man who doesn't like me doing this job. When he hears the *arum-arum-araaagh* of some sexy new V12 throbberchops, he slaps his forehead. His name is Wayne Lawley and he is my political agent. He is the man who gets me elected, and on every other question, I would defer to his advice.

Wayne thinks that the trouble with the Tory party is that we are seen as overprivileged twats. He says we are out of

Could I really drive the Murano and expect people to vote Tory?

touch with how 'ordinary' people live their lives, so when I arrive at the doorstep of a constituent in a car worth twice as much as his house, Wayne doesn't think it's very 'man of the people'. He has even requested that I stop appearing at events in *GQ* test cars.

My interpretation of human nature is different from Wayne's. First, I reject the very concept of 'ordinary' people. And second, I think we Tories are at our best when we spurn the politics of envy and mobilise people's aspirations. And what could be more aspirational than this Nissan Murano?

It was delivered to me on the eve of the General Election and as soon as I saw it, I chuckled. 'Tee hee,' I said to myself as I took in the ludicrously arrogant Darth Vader-style snout. What was it saying, with the plutocratic sneer of that gleaming grille? It was saying, 'Out of my way, small car driven by ordinary person on modest income. Make way for Murano!' I couldn't wait to see Wayne's reaction. So I fired up the V6 engine and headed for Henley to woo the electorate.

Before we had gone forward an inch, I hit on one of the Murano's slickest features. When I reversed out of my parking place, I discovered that there on the dashboard is a live film of whatever is going on under your rear bumper. It's sensational. If you happen to run over your neighbour's Pekinese, you have a snuff movie of the event. Or suppose a crazed Murano-hater is crouched behind you, stuffing bananas up your twin exhaust. You will see him in your CCTV, shortly before you run him over.

The Murano is even better going forward, as fast as any Mercedes and, with its 18-inch, six-spoke alloy wheels, as proud of the ground as any SUV. The closer I got to Wayne, the more apprehensive I became. You should have seen the CD player, the flash sat-nav, the pouches for drinks and phones … Could I really drive this around and expect people to vote Tory? Years ago, I had a lift in the car of the Lib Dem's Vince Cable, and it seemed the perfect vote winner: frugal, modest and full of pamphlets on Third World debt. And then there was me in this evil-grilled Japanese monster …

When I arrived at Henley constituency's HQ, Wayne was coming out with the agenda for the day. I braced myself. He took one look at me. He looked at the car.

'Nice,' he said. Was he joking? No, he was serious. The best thing about the Murano was that Wayne liked it, and with Wayne onside, who can lose? We launched the campaign in that Murano, and I am happy to say that it did not seem to affect the outcome.

LOTUS POSITION

With the head-turning pulling power
of the Lotus Exige S2 as his wing
man, Boris goes speed dating.

When I was about 12 something terrible happened. I was taken away from a mixed-sex school on the Continent, where I had been in love, and sent to an all-boys prep school in Sussex. I used to sit there pining for her, and wondering whether I would ever have a girlfriend again.

Like most of us, I developed an obsession with the under-matron who was called Jane. Jane was big and bouncy and beautiful and one day I almost passed out when she joined us in the swimming pool in an orange bikini. But the deeper my passion became, the more hopeless I knew it was.

The Exige is the swishest, fastest and most chick-pulling Lotus ever made.

What could I offer her? I was 12, and puberty was wafting her oily hand over my face. Jane was at least 20, and we did not have much in common. I would think of reasons for attending her clinic. I would stand in line, summoning up the courage to get her to examine this strange growth in my groin; and when it was my turn, I would stammer some rubbish about flat feet, and she would send me on my way with a maddeningly saucy remark.

How, I wondered, could I possibly make myself attractive to this sex goddess? How did any man ever attract any woman?

One Sunday morning the school was taking a break from Greek verbs to read the papers, and I heard one of the games masters say something interesting. 'Gor!' he said, flipping the *Sunday Telegraph* mag around so we could all see it. 'Look at that. That's the thing for pulling the girls.'

I stared at the advert, and I can still see it in my mind, and I can hear that phrase: 'pulling the girls'. Here was the means of ending my misery!

It was a picture of a Lotus, and with it was its creator, and if my memory is correct he was called Chapman. I looked at its wide-flared bonnet, the obvious speed and audacity of its design. I began to fantasise about how things might be.

The picture of the car swirled before me, and suddenly it was a summer evening, and the rest of the school was in Chapel. Or having yet more Greek verbs thrashed into them with a Jokari bat. At any rate, I had eluded my captors, and was at the wheel of the Lotus, scrunching up the gravel outside the under-matron's quarters.

Jane came out. She gave a gasp, and soon she was by my side and we were tooling through the woods of the Home Counties until we came to a bosky nook, then ...

Then I came to my senses, partly because I was foggy about what happens next, but mainly because I was struck by the impossibility of it all. I would never have a Lotus, I thought. Girls like Jane would always be beyond my reach, I whimpered.

That is why it was such a huge moment when two of the biggest cheeses in the Lotus group came to my office to hand over the swishest, fastest, most chick-pulling Lotus ever devised.

'Just look down here,' said one of them, digging his fingernail into the tyre of the Exige. 'There's nothing else like it. We make them all soft like that so it sticks to the road.'

'Cool!' I said, while considering the effect the car might have on spectators. Was that games master right? Was this really a lady-pleaser?

'We like this colour very much,' said the Lotus honcho, indicating the amazing shade of tangerine. 'It's very popular.'

'Yeah,' I said, longing for the tutorial to end and for the practical to begin.

Driving a Lotus Exige is like making love to a beautiful woman.

Then they talked about the downward drag the car produced, which is apparently the equivalent of a small rhino standing on your toe and essential to stop the car taking off.

'Right,' I said, and at last they'd given me the keys, and I was off. After almost three decades of frustration, I was finally at the wheel of a Lotus, and boy, I intended to have some fun.

All the way to Oxfordshire I sat contented, and brooded on the effect my machine was having on the female sex. Owing to the low-slung cabin, it was impossible to see their faces as I fizzed past, but I could imagine.

How could anyone remain unmoved by a

car with such fantastic road holding, and with such acceleration that you can weave through the traffic faster than the needle of a seamstress in a Filipino sweatshop?

Breathless and stunned, I pulled into the car park at Tesco in Henley where I had to give a speech. I heard a voice. A female voice.

'Wow!' she said. 'That is some machine. Can I have a go in that?'

I preened, and levered myself out with a leer. 'Of course,' I said.

'When I was a gal, before the war, we used to have such fun in cars like this,' said my new girlfriend, and she got off her disabled tricycle and I helped her in.

Yup: the Lotus Exige – it pulls 'em all right, whatever their age.

Vital statistics

With its mid-engine mounting, huge spoiler and barely legal super-slick tyres, the Exige is a street-legal racing car that would give a supercar a run for its money.

Engine Four cylinder 1,796cc
Performance 0–60mph in 4.9 secs, top speed 147mph
Price (2006) £29,995

Only the testosterone-fuelled Dodge Ram could help Boris Johnson from the mire at the end of a humiliating day's shooting.

PIQUE
PERFORMANCE

Good Lord, I thought, when I saw the size of the thing. The Tarmac buckled beneath about three tonnes of American tariff-protected steel. There was enough rubber to fashion *préservatifs* for the entire student population of Britain, and the whole monstrous dreadnought was coated with enough red varnish to lacquer the nails of every secretary in China. What in the name of Moses was Motown thinking of? Who were they aiming at when they commissioned the Dodge Ram?

This vehicle was a great big red-necked, plaid-shirted, Bud-guzzling, gun-toting, Bush-voting, abortion-hating, electric chair-loving, churchgoing, turkey-shooting statement of the right of every freeborn American to bear arms.

OK, I thought, as I ascended to the cabin, a romper room full of grey leather and cup holders: so this car is meant to be a statement. That statement is I Am Big. But who, I wondered, would feel it necessary to make that point with such outlandish hyperbole? I fired her up and we trundled into the traffic, and as I stared ahead I had a vague impression of objects disappearing far beneath us, out of my line of vision: pigeons, cyclists, bollards, small Korean

cars. It was like being at the bridge of a
hovercraft, and it handled like a big red bar
of soap. When we got to those traffic lights
in London's Regent's Park, and I hit the
accelerator and turned right, the thing fish-
tailed like a car chase from *The Dukes of
Hazzard*. And it was at that moment that I
began to guess the intended market. That
massive red steel flat-bed at the back:
what was it for? It was for putting the deer
in, of course.

That was what this vehicle was: it was a
great big red-necked, plaid-shirted, Bud-
guzzling, gun-toting, Bush-voting, abortion-
hating, electric chair-loving, churchgoing,
turkey-shooting statement of the right of
every freeborn American to bear arms.
It was intended to be driven by the very
Pennsylvania steelworkers who produced
its frozen rivers of metal: the kind of super-
macho characters who ended up blowing
their brains out playing Russian roulette
in Vietnam. It was a hunting car and the
perfect accompaniment for my mission
the following day.

I had to go blamming the poor pheasants
with a friend who was both extremely posh
and rich. The Ram would be just the thing
to arrive in, I thought, and by the end of the
day I was very glad I did. The trouble with
shooting is that every time I accept an
invitation, I forget that a) I haven't got the
right gear, b) I haven't got a gun and c) I
couldn't hit a barn door, and so when I
rolled up late for the first drive, my nerves
were already jangling with anticipated
embarrassment.

I entered the baronial chamber in which

the sportsmen had foregathered, and felt eight pairs of eyes swivel my way. My fellow shooters were ranged about the hearth. One had a glass of buck's fizz half-raised to his lips. One had his foot on the fender of the fire, another was leaning a casual elbow on the chimney-piece. All of them were swaddled in tweed, and as their eyes turned my way, it would be wrong to say that they looked quizzical. They didn't look curious.

In a hotly contested field, I think it might have been one of the most humiliating days of my life.

When they beheld my torn jeans, my boots, my scruffy cord jacket, they looked at me with the frank disgust of the bride's father spying some discredited ex-boyfriend arriving at a wedding not wearing morning dress.

And all day long, my awkwardness increased. Bird after bird sailed on obliviously through the penumbra of my lead; and at the end of every drive my companions would smile pityingly at the 50 spent cartridges I left by my peg, and the single bird that fell to my gun, and at last, in the gloaming of the final drive, there occurred my crowning indignity.

I was standing next to my host. 'There you go, Boris!' he shouted, as the last bird of the day lolloped into an unmissable position above my gun. Blam! Blam! A branch detached itself from the tree and fell on to my host's head, and the pheasant flapped to freedom. At which point my boots lost their grip in the mud, and I fell prone, burying my friend's Purdey in the mulch.

In a hotly contested field, I think it might have been one of the most humiliating days of my life: except that as we walked back, everyone saw the Dodge. It was so much huger than their cars, so obviously eloquent of pointless and preposterous testosterone, that in that glorious moment all the pain of the day was suddenly gone. 'Is that your car?' said a soft, incredulous voice.

'It is,' I said. That is the point of the Dodge Ram.

Vital statistics

The Dodge Ram SRT-10 will only be available in left-hand drive and if you can get double-figure miles per gallon, consider yourself lucky.

Engine 8.3-litre V10 (500bhp)
Performance 0–60mph in 5.6 secs, top speed 155mph
Price (2006) £37,995

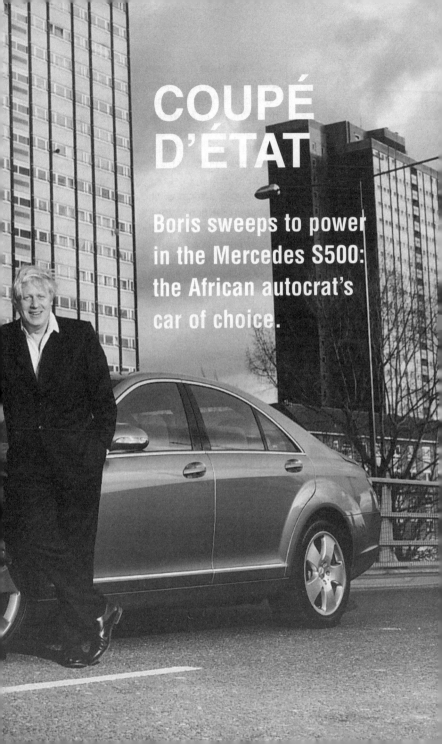

COUPÉ D'ÉTAT

Boris sweeps to power in the Mercedes S500: the African autocrat's car of choice.

The next time the brand managers at Mercedes are struggling to name its new *über*-car, I have the solution. Never mind Kompressor or all these numbers beginning with SL. Let's be honest, folks, and name the big machine after its real target market. Let's just call it the Mercedes Diktator and be done with it, because we all know that the Merc is the car of choice for the discerning African tyrant.

The bigger the jerk, the bigger the Merc, and when I took the new S-class saloon on a 400-mile round trip to Exeter, I began to understand why.

The bigger the jerk, the bigger the Merc.

As the outskirts of London flitted by, I felt my skin darkening, my nostrils flaring, my eyes acquiring a pair of figurative shades, and I was psychologically morphing into a member of the WaBenzi, the elite band of Merc-driving thugs who rule Africa. Pillowed as I was in the luxury of the cabin, caressed in the embrace of a seat with as many positions as the *Kama Sutra*, I started to feel a sense of distance between myself and the poverty-stricken population outside.

Idi Amin had three Mercedes-Benzes, Jean-Bédel Bokassa had 15, Mobutu Sese Seko of Zaire had six for his summer house, and when Samuel Doe seized power in Liberia he splurged on 60 of the German-built cars. The socialist tyrant Robert Mugabe bought dozens of S320s and E240s for his wife and ministers, and is driven in a colossal SL600 that weighs five tons, does two kilometres to the gallon and has to be followed by a tanker in a land now almost dry of petrol; and he buys the Merc because no other machine so perfectly expresses his supremacy.

As I looked out at Ealing through the coup-proof, Kalashnikov-resistant windows, I was seized by that Mugabe-ish sense of autocracy, of indifference to the little people. The landscape became a hot hell of flies and dust, and shanty shops with hopeless hand-painted advertising, and worryingly thin people squatting by the road and listlessly passing their hands over their faces, and yipping pie-dogs fleeing my onset.

And I was a tyrant, with a Luger in the glove compartment, and one of my wives or mistresses squealing with pleasure at the squeeze she got from the electronic seat every time I cornered on the potholed roads. And in the leather-upholstered back were the lads with the AK-47s, ready to blaze behind us when I showed the political opposition one of the key qualities of this machine – not just power, and grace, and authority, but cheetah-like acceleration.

Later on, when we'd escaped death again, we'd have a few Tusker beers and use the Merc to interrogate the traitor we suspected of giving away our route. First we'd lock him in and turn down the air con until it was colder than anything experienced in Africa; and if he survived that we'd jam his head in the sunroof and decapitate him, or put him in the rear

Vital statistics

According to Mercedes-Benz studies, the S500 offers such a relaxing ride that drivers have a heart rate approximately six per cent lower than owners of other luxury motors.

Engine 5,461cc, V8
Performance 0–62mph in 5.4 secs, limited to 155mph
Price (2006) £69,815

footwell and recline the front seats until he was bent out of shape, or maybe we'd play James Blunt on the stereo until he was begging to be shot.

Yes, the more you look at the new Mercedes – and, in all seriousness, it is one of the best cars I have ever driven – the clearer it is why the world's maniacs

As I looked out through the coup-proof, Kalashnikov-resistant windows I was seized by that Mugabe-ish sense of autocracy, of indifference to the little people.

are so in love with them. Even the good guys are smitten: Nelson Mandela was offered an SL600 and accepted it; Thabo Mbeki was offered an identical beast for a test drive and failed to return it for six months. In the same year Britain decided to increase aid to Malawi, its government celebrated by spending £1.7m on – guess what – 39 new Mercedes. All of which is seized upon by those who think aid is a waste of money.

See what happens! They say aid money is just poor people in rich countries paying for the cars of rich people in poor countries, and who can deny they have a point? All I can say is, if you want to feel like a dictator, if you want to feel that you

are at the wheel of a substantial proportion
of your country's overseas earnings, then
invest in a Merc. And if you do, by the way,
you should know it is not just the dictators
of Africa who are now buying the Stuttgart
machines. The growing African middle class
are also deciding on Mercs, and wisely, too,
because they are one of the few cars so
well built as to be able to keep their value
on the continent's appalling roads.

And is it such a bad thing that ambitious
Africans should drive these magnificent
creations? Is it too much to hope they will
be inspired to emulate the Mercedes
themselves? One day, we must pray, cars
like the Merc will be not just driven in Africa,
but made there, too.

NIGHT RIDER

Boris sets off on a nocturnal gallop through southern England behind the wheel of the feisty new Ferrari F430.

Oh no, I thought. Not again. Not a-bloody-gain. It was well after midnight, and I was somewhere on the Somerset–Wiltshire border, and the light on the Ferrari dashboard was telling me that I was about to run out of petrol.

With the dispassionate certainty of some doom-bearing Harley Street cardiologist, the Ferrari's electronics were telling me that I was about to cark it, and I have learned from experience that the dashboard doesn't lie. These Ferraris have no reserve tank. One moment you are growling along, looking for a petrol station, the next, it's pocka-pocka phut.

The last time it happened was about 6.30pm in the fast lane of the A40, and I had to be pushed by two policemen, amid the derision of the entire traffic jam. But now I was stuck on the A303, in desolate Wiltshire, and as I passed one boarded-up gas station after another, the dashboard light seemed ever more insistent.

Desperately I stared into the blackness. Sweat dewed my brow. I braced myself for the humiliation ahead. I would have to hitch a lift from a truck-driving psychopath to the nearest 24-hour services, walk to the counter in my black tie, buy a jerrycan … oh the shame. What made it worse was that I hadn't even had a chance to give the Ferrari F430 a good gallop. I'd driven it that afternoon from London to Exeter, and all the way the great beast had been hemmed in by traffic, like some racehorse trying to weave through a herd of cows. It was true that I'd had *some* fun, and I'd started to understand how to drive a Ferrari.

The essence of it, in my view, is not to change up until you hit about 6,000 revs, and then it feels so beautifully smooth. There is a tiny click from the paddles, and then the car surges forward obediently, as though it was just waiting to be asked. Yet every time I had got it up to galloping speed, I'd hit a wall of red-tail-lighted ruminants and had to slow down.

A full tank and an open road is all you need to get to know the Ferrari F430's thoroughbred grace.

It had been thoroughly frustrating, and now, instead of a glorious burn-up, I was pathetically puttering and peering and praying, praying and peering and – Allah be praised! An oasis!

It was as though the whole county of Hampshire was lying back and opening her well-bred legs to be ravished by the Italian stallion.

At Amesbury I found a huge new services, brightly lit, empty and selling everything from condoms to cut flowers. I bought some chewing gum, clamped my mitts to the leather of the steering wheel, and decided to see why they make such a fuss of the Ferrari F430.

A hundred miles later, I understood. The reason I like riding a bike in London is that you have a sense of freedom that belongs to no one else on the road. You can see a point 20 yards ahead, and direct your machine there at exactly the speed and time of your choosing. The same principle, at much greater speeds and distances, applies to the late-night Ferrari.

Suppose you come off the roundabout in second, and the dual carriageway opens ahead. You can see the lights of the lorry half a mile ahead, and you can see the exact ribbon of Tarmac that you're going to occupy as you overtake, and though the road is uphill and arcing to the left, you know that in only a few seconds you are going to get there and, roar-click, you take it up until you hit top gear, and as you swirl past the lorry you may want that extra ounce of power and control, to ricochet round the bend, so you click down to fifth and listen to the ecstatic bubble from the exhaust, until the revs climb from 5,500 to 6,000 and it's time to take it through the roof again.

There was one glorious passage when I seemed to be averaging a speed of X*, and then the M3 opened up before me, a long quiet Bonneville flat stretch, and I am afraid it was as though the whole county of Hampshire was lying back and opening her well-bred legs to be ravished by the Italian stallion. To hell with it, I thought: and I recorded a speed of X**.

Later on, after punching through that sound barrier, I understood how speed and sensation are so relative. I found I was travelling at X***, and felt I was only dawdling. That is how the Ferrari turns its drivers into addicts.****

Vital statistics

The F430 is the first Ferrari with the *manettino* – an F1-style switch on the steering wheel controlling five different driving settings.

Engine 4.3-litre V8
Performance 0–60mph in 4 secs, top speed 196mph
Price (2006) £121,750

---

* For the speed, take the number of virgins that suicide bombers expect to find in paradise, double it, then subtract the percentage of 18- to 30-year-olds in higher education in 1964.
** The number of Athenian survivors of the battle of Marathon, minus the sons of Abijah and the wives of Henry VIII.
*** The number of UK higher education institutions, minus Charles Moore's age.
**** Memo to cops: this review is essentially a work of fiction.

RAFT OF OPTIONS

Boris finds there's nothing finer than messing about on the river … especially in a Dutton Commander Amphijeep.

H2O DUT

'**OK Boris,**' said the *GQ* photographer.

'This is it!'

He was standing on the dock, waving me forward and making noises of genuine excitement. 'This is the money shot!' he said.

In just a few moments we were due for the moment of penetration, the moment I had been waiting for most of my life.

I was gonna dip my wick. I was gonna wet my prow. I was going to baptise my bonnet in Mother Nature's bodily fluid.

Half-boat, half-car, half-mad – the Dutton Commander S2 1,300cc Amphijeep inched in first gear towards the slipway.

The Dutton – half-boat, half-car, half-mad.

Before us was the river. Strong. Green. Fast-flowing. Mysterious.

Two miles downstream, it was nearing lunchtime on the Friday of the Henley Regatta.

The world's greatest aquatic athletes were approaching the climax of their exertions.

By now the mob would be verging on maximum exaltation.

Thousands of blazers. The flower of English womanhood. Pissed.

Now was the moment for the MP to pull off his *coup de théâtre*. Now was the time to accept the roars of derision and delight.

I was gonna be a James Bond-style hero. If only I could stay afloat.

I eased off the brake and the clutch,

and five feet, four, three, two, one …

Now the front wheels were skidding in the lapping swan effluent at the bottom of the slipway; now they were under.

On and down and suddenly *sploooosh*. *GQ* had its money shot.

As the poet Springsteen puts it, we went down to the river, and into the river we drove, and after a yard or two we had changed identity.

We morphed. We pupated. We slipped the surly bonds of land and became a boat.

I did something clever with the levers, and the engine switched to two jets at the back, and now we were chugging through the sweet soft Thames, and after we repeated the exercise and picked up my crew, we headed for the Regatta.

If the world has anything lovelier than the river in the first weeks of July, I would be obliged if readers could let me know.

The foliage of the oak and the alders is at its fullest. There are black tenebrous pools where it hangs over the water.

As the salmon and the trout lay dappled in their files, noses pointed upstream, they must have seen something marvellous. A car passed overhead, a car with four tyres.

How the hell, you may ask, can an Amphijeep make progress like that, with the wheels dragging through the water?

You have a point. There are certainly plenty of other amphibious vehicles which do not have Tim Dutton's robust approach to design. You may have seen them in the movies.

There is something called the Gibbs Aquada, for instance, which can do more than 100mph on land and 30 knots in the water, thanks to a hydroplane system.

Flat out – and we were going flat out – the Dutton does about five and a half knots.

In fact, Dutton himself explained some law of physics that means the more you floor the throttle, the more bow-wave resistance you build up, and the slower you go.

Well, who cares? The Dutton is significantly cheaper (from £29,950) than its so-called competitors. And as the maximum permissible speed on this stretch of the Thames is eight knots, anything swisher would not only be vulgar but also illegal.

By now we were attracting some acclaim.

Revellers hailed us from their pleasure cruisers. Out of their launches came nut-brown Henley housewives, beaming broadly in their bikinis.

We waved back, though frankly I was reluctant to take my hands off the wheel. The steering in the water is tricky.

It takes at least 20 yards to respond to a yank on the wheel, so the beginner is constantly correcting and over-correcting.

Indeed, it was partly our zigzag course that was prompting the cheers from the bank, and when we came to the lock we collided with a boat called *Myrtle*.

Now Henley was in sight. We could see the church. We could see the candy-striped marquees and hear the roars.

At once I had a vision of the Dutton sinking the umpires' launch. What if we hit Pinsent or Redgrave? Crunch.

I decided – and you will agree that this was particularly heroic – that I had attracted enough attention for one day.

There on the left was Hobbs' boat yard, complete with slipway.

We lined up the wheels. We came off once. We came off again. At last, with a tremendous roaring and splooshing we emerged from the water amid a forest of craning necks and camera phones.

We stood for a moment, basking in the amazing sensation of driving out of the water. It was like D-Day, like a birth. It was fantastic.

The Dutton. It is neither the car that thinks it's a boat nor the boat that thinks it's a car. It has the invincible superiority of knowing that it is both.

Boris and the Dutton Commander emerge victorious from the river at Henley.

Vital statistics

You need a driver's licence to take the Amphijeep on the road, but not to drive one on the water.

Engine 1,300cc (based on a 4x4 Suzuki Samurai)
Performance 0–60mph in 13 secs, top speed 90mph on land, 6mph on water
Price (2006) £29,950

NUMBER OF THE BEAST

Boris faces his demons and learns how to harness the brute force of Caterham's magnificent Seven.

For the first time in my career as *GQ*'s motoring correspondent, I looked out of the window at the car I was meant to drive, and felt a sense of unease. It was about 6am. It was cold. A biblical rain was falling on north London.

It fell like gunfire on the tinny bonnet of the Caterham Seven. I could almost see it sluicing through the puny tarpaulin that covered the cabin. I knew what this was going to be like.

The previous day I had driven it once around the block, and I had never found a car so skittish, so difficult to bring to heel. This thing goes from 0–60mph in 3.1 seconds, and no matter how gently I eased my left foot off the clutch it would explode forwards like a champagne cork, and then I would instinctively depress the clutch and it would stop again, and then as soon as the left toe came up again it was ka-boing, ka-boing, down the road and around the corner like a coke-crazed kangaroo.

After a while, the car began to submit to my instructions, as a fiery steed acknowledges the bit of a new horseman.

To drive this thing to Oxford would be an act of masochism akin to sitting in a cold tin bath going down a black run surrounded by a chorus of pneumatic drills. I began to think yearningly of my clapped-out old Toyota people-mover: so big, so comfy, so warm, such a doddle to drive.

'Are you really going to use that thing?' asked my wife sleepily. I looked down again at the splayed insect-like form of the Caterham. You wouldn't even notice it if you were the driver of some late-night Eddie Stobart pantechnicon. In the dark and the roar of the road surface water, you could crush it with your off-front wheel and think you'd hit a badger.

'Isn't it a bit dangerous?' she asked, and just as I was about to agree, I thought of the guys at *GQ*, and of my reputation as a man of action. How could I possibly tell them that I'd been put off by a spot of rain? I could not.

'Oh no,' I said. 'It'll be fine.' And of course for the first half hour it wasn't.

It was very far from fine.

I have read somewhere that driving a Caterham Seven is the most fun a man can have with his trousers on. Well, after about five minutes, so much water had leaked through the tarpaulin I would have been better off without trousers at all.

The Caterham Seven is a car with no pretensions to luxury. There are no cup holders. There is no walnut fascia. There is no sat-nav. There's no air conditioning of any description, and as I sat there going ka-boing, ka-boing, ka-boing up the Liverpool Road I felt such hot shame that the placky windows had soon steamed to the point of complete opacity.

At one stage the machine catapulted itself into a roundabout before I had time to

Vital statistics

The new Caterham Seven is the first road car to feature a Cosworth engine in more than ten years.

Engine 4-cylinder, 2,261cc
Performance 0–60mph in 3.1 secs, top speed 155mph
Price (2006) From £31,000

wipe off the mist, and I looked out to see the terrified rictus of a cyclist as he braked. 'Wanker!' he screeched, and it was hard to disagree.

It was the noise that saved me. It was the sheer racket that averted a major prang. The Caterham Seven may not cut much of a profile in the rear-view mirror of a lorry.

I looked out to see the terrified rictus of a cyclist as he braked. 'Wanker!' he screeched, and it was hard to disagree.

But there were enough decibels coming out of that great big reticulated python of an exhaust to warn drivers within the radius of a mile that something sporty was approaching, something with a terrifying power-to-weight ratio, and lurching forward at speeds the motorist himself found hard to predict.

Then, after a while, I started to get the hang of it. The car began to submit to my instructions, as a fiery steed acknowledges the bit of a new horseman. We stopped going ka-boing, as I learned to ride the clutch in the traffic, and then all at once, on the motorway, my sensations started to change.

First it was pleasing to find I could overtake anyone I wanted. Then it was exciting to be sitting down between these four wheels, with my coccyx almost grazing the Tarmac, and to realise that this

Caterham Seven is the nearest thing on the roads to a serious racing car.

It may have only a 2.0-litre engine, and a top speed of 155mph, but that's not the point. It is the very flimsiness of its construction – the thought that had deterred me in the morning rain – that gives it the most astonishing grunt.

Even in sixth you can touch the throttle, and, pow, it will pull past your Beemers and your Mercs, and you cease to worry about the roar of the wind and the flapping of the canopy; and you cease to care about the atmospheric moisture in the cabin.

As I returned in the evening, tired and happy, I waved at the white van full of prisoners being ferried from Highbury Corner Magistrates' Court to prisons across the country. 'Look at this!' I said, and I could feel their sad eyes boring through tinted escape-proof portholes.

'Do your time, my friends,' I urged the poor convicts. 'Go straight, and one day you too could have a car like this!' I couldn't hear their response, of course, but I am sure that if anything can give a man hope, as he pays his debt to society, it is the prospect of one day owning a Caterham Seven.

PAPER CHASE

Read all about it! Top Tory Boris reveals all about Lambo happy-snap pap attack!

I cannot tell you how galling it is – for a column that prides itself on being first with the news of every *GQ* test drive – that the *Sun* has already printed pictures of my latest outing. It has depicted me and my children with the Lamborghini Gallardo Spyder before you *GQ* readers have had the chance to read it yourselves.

I call it a flaming cheek.

There we were, howling up the M6 in the fast lane, and my boys and I were all in a terrific mood. We'd taken the hood down at the Toddington Services. The sun was out. We were going to see the last day of the Test match at Old Trafford. When suddenly we were overtaken by a black Golf, driven rather erratically, on the inside lane, and I became aware that someone in the other car was trying to attract my attention.

It appeared to be a couple of students waving and sticking their thumbs up with a bit of paper reading, 'We love you Boris'. I waved back in a spirit of genial condescension, and was disappointed, a few days later, to learn that the episode had been captured on camera.

The account, needless to say, was tosh. Someone from the RAC was produced, who said that I was 'grossly irresponsible'. Double tosh and tripe.

Here for the first time is the exclusive *GQ* account of that fateful drive …

It all began when we were watching *Top Gear* one Sunday. As in many households, *Top Gear* has replaced evensong as a sacred act of family communion. There was Jeremy Clarkson, whanging the Lambo around his track like a maniac and, as my boys' eyes grew ever rounder and shinier, I started to feel pricklings of envy.

At length, the old mastodon juddered to a halt in front of the camera. His features reassembled themselves from their G-force rictus. 'And this,' he said, gesturing at the wonderful machine, 'is the only one in the country!'

At once my hand leapt sideways like a spastic crab. I picked up the phone.

'Henderson!' I barked at *GQ's* Automotive Industries Editor.

'Yessir?' returned the honest fellow.

'Get me the Lambo,' I said, and within a week it was there. In fact, it was the very machine that Clarkson had been demonstrating, as you could tell by the sagging in the orange upholstery, the scuffing of the tyres and the rather dainty little pair of sunglasses (whose, I wonder?) we found in the glove compartment.

And yet in spite of these minor signs of distress, it was, and is, a fantastic machine.

You know the story of Lamborghini. Back in the early Sixties, old Poppa Lamborghini used to drive a Ferrari, and then the clutch expired. He went in person to see Enzo Ferrari, who told him, as they say in Italian, to go and make a bottom.

This is a terrific insult, in Italian, and Pop Lambo was so incensed that he decided to build his own greenfield factory. So the raging black bull was created to rival the prancing black stallion, and one of the world's great marques was launched.

A great marque, that is, which has produced some seriously dud cars. In the course of many vicissitudes Lamborghini has been owned by, among others, the Indonesians, with not altogether happy results.

It is now owned by the Germans, and you know what? The result is that it works. It is still Italian in its soul. When you take it under a motorway bridge you hear this stupendous noise: not a growl, not a howl, but somewhere between a purr and a roar, and as you put your foot down there is a magic moment when the engine note changes and deepens and all the valves and the sprockets suddenly start singing in harmony like a choir of humming Pavarottis as they prepare to oscillate the windows of Milan cathedral.

As in many households, *Top Gear* has replaced evensong as a sacred act of family communion.

It is Italian in the slinky design that caused it to be voted, in March, the most beautiful car in the world.

But it is German in the electrics. Look at the cool way that carbon-fibre engine cover reaches up and accepts the opening roof, and all in about 20 seconds. Look at the way you can lift the nose of the car, in town, to avoid the Liberal Democrat speed bumps.

It is so easy to drive that you really feel it could be your daily runabout.

Except, of course, that it is so hellishly fast.

But not, unfortunately, so hellishly fast that you'll outrun a couple of Golf-driving students on the M6.

Vital statistics

A button on the Spyder's dash raises or lowers the nose. Perfect for negotiating speed bumps. (According to Lamborghini, Boris didn't test it.)

Engine 10 cylinder, 4,961cc producing 520bhp
Performance 0–62mph in 4.3 secs, top speed 190mph
Price (2006) £115,000

ROAD WARRIOR

It's designed to fend off high explosives, but can the Armoured Range Rover stand up to Boris and an air rifle?

Trying to still my breathing, and trying to keep the barrel absolutely straight, I pointed the gun at the big, black, burly beast. Somewhere in a nearby wood, a pheasant emitted a cark.

Then the air was filled with a tense and expectant silence.

'OK you bastard,' I hissed. 'See how this feels.' I only had one round up the spout, but one round would be enough. I shuffled closer, to perhaps 20ft away, and peered through the telescopic sights. It was getting dark and it was starting to drizzle, and I was confident that I was completely invisible to my prey.

The creature hadn't moved an inch for the past 20 minutes. Vast, pachydermatous, oblivious, four and a half tons of Range Rover was waiting to be shot, and I was the man to do it.

All morning I had been hearing about this vehicle and its amazing robustness. If you happen to be a Russian oligarch who falls foul of Putin, this is the car for you. If you are an Arab sheikh and you are worried about al-Qaeda, you get this Range Rover.

It has so much steel that you could build a Ford Transit out of one of the doors. The windows are not only an inch thick; they don't even open. They have been welded to the rim of what is effectively a huge steel cage.

This Range Rover is designed to resist attacks by sarin, mustard gas, road-side improvised explosive devices and bazookas. If the manual is to be believed, you can open up on it with an AK-47 and have about as much impact as a

Vital statistics

Optional extras include an internal oxygen system, covert emergency lights and anti-tamper exhaust.

Engine 4.4-litre V8
Performance 0–60mph in 9.5 secs, top speed 110mph
Price (2007) from £190,000

peashooter on an elephant's backside.

You could kamikaze-crash a Cessna on the roof, and it wouldn't even buckle. It's said this vehicle's vast flat-drive tyres will take it serenely through just about everything except the London traffic.

According to the hype, it is the ideal vehicle for every political target from George W Bush to the most gaffe-prone Tory Shadow Higher Education Spokesman.

This Range Rover is designed to resist attacks by sarin, mustard gas, road-side improvised explosive devices and bazookas.

The only question in my mind, as I sighted that sucker in my Oxfordshire yard, was whether the hype was true. I was a journalist. I was a fully fledged car correspondent, an expert. I couldn't just swallow this stuff from Range Rover. So all day long I had been brooding about a proper test.

There was no doubt that the car was big and forbidding. That morning we were trying to take some photos on my Islington street when a woman called Meg shot out of her house. 'Shame on you!' she cried. 'How can you drive that thing?'

And it was no use the guy from Range Rover trying to explain that the point of the car was to save the lives of American presidents and Russian oil kings.

'Oh fuck that!' exclaimed Meg, and she started to scoop up organic sludge from the gutter for use in her compost. 'Take it away! It makes me feel nauseous.'

So we took it away, and as I drove one of the children to school we had great fun with the public address system. This car is designed against all sorts of worst-case scenarios, and if you want to negotiate with a bunch of Kalashnikov-toting militiamen at a roadblock without opening the doors, you just use the loudspeaker. So whenever we saw a bunch of kids at a bus stop we would hail them, making sure to use our best Robocop accents.

According to the hype, it is the ideal vehicle for every political target from George W Bush to the most gaffe-prone Tory Shadow Higher Education Spokesman.

'You there!' we would say. 'Yes, you,' we would continue, as the poor kids flinched and stared around. 'Be good today! Work hard and achieve more.'

Then we would trundle on to the next bunch of surly-looking kids. 'Don't steal!' we would say, and they would look up and see this terrifying tinted-windowed vision of armour-clad authority.

That is the image; that is Range Rover's sales pitch. But is it really justified? And as my finger curled now around the trigger I had a sudden moment of panic. In my hands was a lethal weapon, a .177 air rifle.

At least, it was pretty lethal if you were an apple. Only a few minutes ago I had fired at a large Granny Smith, and the results were very nasty. There was a huge exit wound, and for the final second before I fired at the car I had a terrible notion that the whole thing was a con.

The glass would shatter. The alarm would go off. I would get a furious letter from the managing director of Range Rover, copied to the editor of *GQ*.

In fact, it must have been on that thought that I finally squeezed the trigger. The air rifle coughed in the gloom. Crack, the slug flattened itself on the darkened glass, and no, there was not a scratch. 'You win, Range Rover,' I thought.

I was going to fire again, at the paintwork, but then I thought that would be unfair. On the other hand, if I ever get another, I am going to hire a bazooka and let Meg have a go.

CITY SLICKER

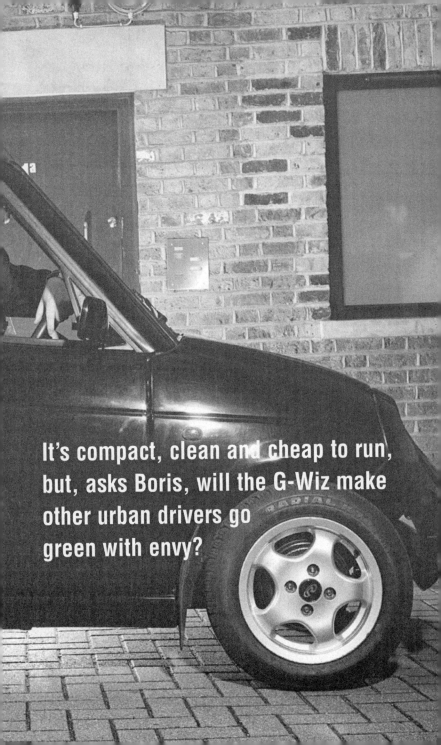

It's compact, clean and cheap to run, but, asks Boris, will the G-Wiz make other urban drivers go green with envy?

There's only one question that really matters about the new G-Wiz. It may have zero emissions. It may be the cleanest, greenest thing in London apart from the windmill-sprouting houses of the Notting Hill Tories. This battery-powered, Indian-assembled saloon may be the hottest thing from Bangalore that doesn't come with poppadoms.

But this column is traditionally called upon to address a very simple issue. For our purposes, it doesn't matter whether a car is as green as pea soup or whether it pumps out more lethal vapours than a field of Holsteins. We only have to satisfy ourselves on one point: is this car really the machine for a red-blooded male?

I was not only saving money, I was saving the planet.

As soon as I saw the little black runabout perched pertly on the pavement I could see why it was just the thing for your alfalfa-munching, *Guardian*-reading, buggy-pushing, conscience-stricken goody-goodies. But what about your average reader of a men's lifestyle magazine, the kind of guy who has – as surveys regularly reveal – testosterone spurting from every pore? Can it conceivably be butch to drive around in this oversized Airfix model?

Let us be blunt: just how *GQ* is the G-Wiz?

Well, folks, I was determined to sneer.

To call it a golf cart would be an insult to the comparatively cougar-like properties of the golf cart. The doors are placky in the extreme. The windows aren't electric. You can't even roll them down. You just shove them open, a feature I seem to remember from my parents' Renault Four in the Seventies.

You can put your foot on the throttle and have that feeling that you must have got the wrong pedal, because for about a second or two there is no response; and only then does the G-Wiz start to move dreamily off with that unhurried gait of a clapped-out dodgem. And yet I have to admit that after a day in the company of the little wheeled rabbit hutch, I was softening; and by the evening I was almost in love.

I had the first insight into her possibilities when I found myself late for a radio interview with nowhere to park. Suddenly I glimpsed half a space – no more than the length of two axe handles – on a meter. That G-Wiz eased her black bottom into the gap, and to complete my joy I saw a couple of parking wardens loping towards me with all the sinister purpose of a brace of hyenas seeing a fallen wildebeest.

'What is it?' they asked, sniffing around the G-Wiz, and starting to tap on their huskies.

'It's electric,' I explained, and got back in to show them what I meant. I turned the key, and nothing happened; and that was the point. There was no noise of an engine starting, but the G-Wiz was already running.

When I pulled silently out, their eyes widened like African tribesmen seeing a plane for the first time.

I parked again and beamed. 'See?' I said. 'OK,' they said. 'It's electric. It pays nothing.'

I have to admit that after a day in the company of the little wheeled rabbit hutch, I was softening; and by the evening I was almost in love.

That is the way to a city motorist's heart, and as the day went on I started to feel ever more virtuous, ever more *right*. Oh, I know there will be plenty of people out there who are cynical about global warming, and who think it is just a kind of stone-age religion.

And it is rather like a religion, in that everybody gets very hysterical, and calls for acts of sacrifice and propitiation of the sun-god – and yet we haven't got a clue whether our sacrifices will make any difference. But as world religions go, I like global warming. If it brings humanity together in a common purpose, and it makes us concentrate on all the pollution we are making, then it can't be altogether a bad thing.

By the end of the day I was in a happy little trance. I beetled down alleyways that would have been impassable to my great

big fat Toyota. I crept up silently behind
people and tooted my little horn. I found that
it really could go quite fast downhill; and let
me tell you, it doesn't matter a damn that
the top speed is only 42mph when the
average speed of London traffic is 3mph.

And all the time I was warming the
cockles of my heart with the thought that it
was so damn *cheap*. It seems to cost about
50p to charge the batteries for a 40-mile
round trip. Only a bicycle beats that. And
not only was I saving money – I was saving
the planet!

As I tootled along I composed a very
feeble kind of clerihew: If you drive a G-Wiz/
The theory is/The world will be cooler/Than
if you drive a Roller.

I haven't a clue if that is the case, but the
G-Wiz is a lovely gizmo and well worth
every penny of £7,000. The surprising thing
is that they have only sold less than 1,000
of them.

I can't believe more thrusting *GQ* types
haven't already rushed out to get one,
because the really great thing is that you
can park it at the back of the garage and
still leave plenty of room for the
Lamborghini.

Vital statistics

The G-Wiz costs about
1.3p per mile to run. It's
exempt from road tax,
the Congestion Charge
and free to park on
meters in Westminster
and the City.

Engine Electric
Performance 0–60mph
– you wish, top speed
42mph
Price (2007) £6,999

FANCY A SPIN

Hoping to impress a young researcher, Boris transforms himself into an Alfa Romeo Spider-man.

You need to drive this beautiful little machine for a few hours before you understand the central mystery.

Why is it called a Spider?

The Alfa Romeo Spider is a very heavy 3.2-litre marvel.

I mean, it is obvious why the VW Beetle is called a beetle. It has a domey kind of carapace, and it beetles along in such a way that you could easily visualise it nosing a ball of dung down the road. The same could be said of the de Havilland Mosquito, the wartime plane that bore a clear resemblance to its insect eponym. The Mosquito whined through the night, unseen and terrifying. Then 'dugga, dugga, peeow', you got stung, especially if your name was Jerry.

And when the Italians called their motor scooters Vespas, or wasps, the metaphor was equally comprehensible. Just go to Brighton and watch the mods all buzzing and swarming around, and you get the point. But the Alfa Romeo Spider seems to bear no physical or spiritual resemblance whatever to an eight-legged creature. I've brooded on this question for many years. At one point I thought it might have been a simple error of translation. I have read somewhere that Nissan wanted to give its new 4x4 a vaguely cowboy feel, so it called it a Pajero, without realizing that it was the Spanish for 'wanker'. Perhaps someone at

Alfa misread his English phrase book, back there in the late Fifties when the car was first conceived. Perhaps he got 'spider' jumbled up with the word for some other creature more famous for its speed.

Perhaps he was thinking of 'fly'. This vroomy V6 doesn't inch itself sideways. There is no hint of a scuttle. It shoots forward like a dart: like a turbocharged 260bhp soap dish, designed by Pininfarina. This Spider has four butch alloy wheels – not eight spindly legs.

I was still trying to work it out as we drove to Oxford to check out some university facilities. When I say we, I mean myself and my new 21-year-old researcher. The trouble about having a 21-year-old

The Alfa Romeo Spider 3.2 Q4 was named Best Cabriolet of the Year at the 2006 Geneva Motor Show and, following tradition, the retractable roof is made of fabric.

researcher, when you reach my age, is that you want to show her the driving savoir-faire that has entrenched my position as one of *GQ*'s premier motoring correspondents.

So we yee-hahed up the M40 like a bat out of hell – a bat, you note, not a spider out of hell. We overtook on the outside and we overtook on the inside. We accelerated from nought to 62 in seven seconds. It was tremendous. I had the feeling that she was probably impressed.

Now that I was not showing off, I was overcome by the charm of the car, and the Spider began to weave her magic …

It is a measure of the robustness of the modern Alfa that in the course of showing off I managed to engage reverse gear at a very fast speed. And survive. But in what sense was it spider-like?

I showed the researcher how the hood went up and down in 27 seconds. That is rather faster than I am able to brush my teeth, tie my shoelaces or perform a number of other tasks these days. It was miraculous – but if you were called upon to name a bug that could do the same sort of thing, you might nominate the ladybird, perhaps, but not an arachnid.

Why not the Alfa Romeo Ladybird?

I was still turning the problem over as I drove home with the sun behind me. Now I was alone in the car, my researcher having

mysteriously decided to take the bus from
Oxford. As I hummed peaceably through the
countryside, I thought of the illustrious
history of the Spider. Of course the car has
evolved almost out of all recognition. This is
a very heavy 3.2-litre marvel, groaning with
electronics.

The modern Alfa Spider has as much in
common with the Alfa Spider driven by
Dustin Hoffman in *The Graduate* as the
aircraft carrier *Ark Royal* has in common
with the ship of that name launched by
Elizabeth I. And yet I felt the spell of the
brand take effect. Slowly, now that I was not
showing off, I was overcome by the charm
of the car, and the Spider began to weave
her magic …

And then, yes … *weave* … I got it.

It's called a spider because it's a cunning
kind of girl car, and she takes us poor men
into her embrace and spins a lovely net
around us with her gossamer filaments. She
seduces the driver, the Alfa Romeo Spider,
and we step right ahead in her web.

Vital statistics

Engine 3.2-litre, 260bhp
V6
Performance 0–60mph
in 7.0 secs, top speed
149mph
Price (2007) £31,250

GOING MOBILE

Ladies and gentlemen, as a Tory MP who seeks to modernise his party, it is time for me to make a confession.

I belong to a minority, a group reviled across middle Britain for our unnatural behaviour. So many people already suspect me of belonging to this minority, so many people have caught me at it, that I can no longer bear, quite frankly, to cover it up.

For too long, I and my kind have kept our preferences in the dark, and in this bright, kind, inclusive, touchy-feely new universe, it would be hypocritical of me to hide it from you any more.

It is not only that I belong to that pathetic and dwindling minority of straight, white, married, middle-class, corpulent, Old Etonian moderate smokers and drinkers. This admission is far worse. My friends, I am a cyclist.

I am a member of that hated minority that rides a bicycle. We are the object of a particularly virulent and nasty prejudice, and deserve the fullest protection from the coarser instincts of the rest of society. Seldom have I felt the sting of disapproval, or the threat to my way of life, more keenly than yesterday; and what made it worse was that my attacker was not a pedestrian, or a motorist. She was another cyclist, what we must call a self-hating cyclist.

There I was, trundling up Liverpool Road, and using my bike as my office, when the enemy overtook. You know who I mean by the enemy: the kind of bossy, Islingtonian female who becomes a health minister in the New Labour Government.

It is not only that I belong to that pathetic and dwindling minority of straight, white, married, middle-class, corpulent, Old Etonian moderate smokers and drinkers. This admission is far worse.

She was wearing the fluorescent yellow zig-zag things, and cycle clips, and her streamlined helmet was properly strapped beneath her chin. She knew that I was threat neither to her nor to any other person on that virtually deserted road. And yet, as she stertorously overhauled me, in the drizzle, she yelled – howled – 'Don't talk on your mobile phone!'

I am afraid I was in the middle of a particularly tricky conversation and, though I am mild-mannered, I responded tersely. At which point, she pulled up and waited, glowering, for me to catch up.

Uh-oh, I thought, now it's bike rage.

She's going to bean me with her pump. 'It's utterly disgraceful,' she cried, 'that you should be doing this when you are a Tory MP, and when it is illegal.' As it happens, since I am fully aware of my responsibilities, I have studied the position, and I know that my actions were perfectly legal.

'Well,' she shouted, 'it soon will be illegal!' On the contrary, I told her, among the many political tasks I have set myself is to prevent the practice from ever being outlawed by parliament. Just as I will never vote to ban hunting, so I will never vote to abolish the free-born Englishman's time-hallowed and immemorial custom, dating back as far as 1990 or so, of cycling while talking on a mobile.

'But you are in charge of a vehicle,' said the self-appointed tyrant. Yes, I said: she was right, but I was perfectly capable of weaving my wobbling way with one hand to my ear. Suppose I were scratching my head. There is no law that says you must have both hands on the handlebars at all times, and it would be madness if there were. What if I had no left hand at all?

It strikes me that her objection to one-handed cycling is, prima facie, against the principles of modern anti-discrimination law. What did she have to say to that, eh? She had nothing to say, because she had already pedalled furiously on.

I meditated, as I looked at her angry back, on the difference between my temperament and hers. It is true that my habit may involve some tiny but appreciable increase in the risk of an accident. Many people would not dream of doing it, and no one would recommend it for those mad cyclists who pump around in Lycra at terrifying speed, their legs and arms like chiselled mahogany whippets.

Nor do I propose to defend the right to talk on a mobile while driving a car, though I don't believe that is necessarily any more dangerous than the many other risky things that people do with their free hands while driving – nose-picking, reading the paper, studying the A–Z, beating the children, and so on.

Uh-oh, I thought, now it's bike rage. She's going to bean me with her pump.

The salient point is that, in the case of both cycling and driving, dangerous and erratic behaviour is more than adequately covered by existing law. If the police think you are driving carelessly, and are not in control of your vehicle, they can haul you over and fine you on the spot; and talking on a mobile, while driving, is already grounds enough for such punishment.

But, in the course of lengthy consultations, the police have made it clear that they do not want to be obliged, by law, to take such steps in every case; and they should, perhaps, be heeded. All the same, before millions write in and belabour me with road death statistics from Holland and Canada, let me repeat: I speak here only for cyclists, and will defend their right to cycle and phone while there is breath in my body.

The lady who assailed me on the way to work yesterday was wrong about the law; and the more I think about the harmlessness of my methods – hugging the kerb, just as ships in the ancient world used to hug the coast of the Mediterranean – the clearer it is that she wasn't really interested in road safety. She simply felt a hatred, a stark, insensible hatred, at watching a chap enjoying the use of a technology that did not exist 20 years ago.

I hope she doesn't get her new law, and that we still give cyclists the freedom to choose to take the infinitesimal risks involved. I think that is civilisation. She thinks it is barbarism. She thinks only the law can restrain people like me. I say: *corruptissima republica, plurimae leges*.

MOTORISTS, REVOLT: ME, I'M ON MY BIKE

My friends, I am a doomed man. If I read this latest letter correctly, I am on the point of losing the right to drive.

The state will shortly take away from me the privilege I first earned at the age of 18, when, after massive investment in the British School of Motoring, I passed my driving test first time.

Since then, I have driven many hundreds of thousands of miles, in dozens of countries, and never yet had a prang. Not a single person has been thrown from my bumper; not a deer, not a cat, not a dog, not even, dare I say it, a mouse.

If you discount the minor flesh wound sustained by a Cornish meat pie van that brushed my Alfa very late at night some years ago, I have barely come into physical contact with another vehicle, so scrupulous is my driving.

Wherever I go, I see louts who pull out without looking, who overtake on blind corners, who fling open their doors just as

I am coming by on my bicycle.

I see idiots and crash-artists and prangmeisters and fools who change nappies on the hard shoulder; and in all this carnival of incompetence and carelessness it is I – I, who have never so much as crunched a headlight! I, who have never even stoved in a bonnet, boot or door! – I am being taken off the road.

According to my secretary, Batley-born Ann Sindall, I have now been photographed so often by the same speed camera, exceeding the speed limit by the same pathetic amount, that, come September, the game will be up.

She has been counting the letters from the police, and totting up the points. The emanations of the state will be warned that I am no longer allowed on the Queen's highway, and any breach of the ban will be an imprisonable offence.

I don't know what technical advance is responsible, but speed cameras are now like the most ruthless of tabloid paparazzi: they get you every time.

But it's not fair! I wail to her. I'm a safe driver, I whimper; and she just chuckles, like Dick Dastardly's dog, Muttley.

'Eeeyup,' she says, 'the law's the law.' And, of course, she is right. In so far as speed cameras save lives, there is no arguing against them.

It is all very well launching into some libertarian rant against the oppressions of the state, and J Bonington Jagsworth's basic right to drive, but just you try it on someone who has lost a relative because some berk was going too fast.

Insofar as speed cameras restore some measure of tranquillity to villages cursed by a fast road, they must be a good thing. If speed cameras could ensure that country roads were safe enough for children to cycle on, I'd have Gatsos on every signpost.

We drivers must simply accept that speed cameras have changed the meaning of the signs by the side of the road. When it says 50, it is no longer meant to be an indicative sort of number, like 'Drinks, 6.30pm'.

It means that, if you go above 50mph, you will not only be in breach of the law, but you will also be punished for breaching the law in cruel and material ways. If, for instance, you write a motoring column for *GQ* magazine, you will have your livelihood taken away.

We drivers must accept that these cameras are no longer Potemkin objects, as they seemed to be for the first few years, empty scarecrows with no film in them.

I don't know what technical advance is responsible, but the cameras are now like the most ruthless of tabloid paparazzi: they get you every time.

It is precisely because they are so effective, and because technology has so emphatically given the state the whip hand over the motorist, that I now ask you, ladies and gentlemen of the jury, whether you feel that the punishments need to be adjusted.

You may feel that this is special pleading from a man who faces the prospect of being forced to go to and from his constituency by train. Well, I suppose I had better put my hands up to that.

It is time for the jackboot to come off the neck of the motorist.

But I have reason to think that I am not alone in my bitterness. The other day, I was with a group of parents watching *Johnny English* and, though the children laughed like drains at the lavatory gags, there was only one moment when the adults all cheered and punched the air, and that was when the special agent's supercar destroys a speed camera with a Sidewinder missile.

These cameras are bringing misery and uncertainty to many people who are safe drivers, and who depend on their cars, and the cameras do this because their sheer efficiency means the punishment is disproportionate to the crime.

You fail a handful of times to ease up at the same camera, and bang, you've lost your licence.

Let us by all means use the cameras to enforce the speed limit; let us continue to allow local authorities to locate the cameras where they choose, under the rules allowed by the law.

But let us be honest that these cameras

are at least partly there to raise revenue – 50 per cent of the cash goes to the Treasury and, though there has been a fourfold increase in their use since 1997, the number of deaths on the road has remained static; and given that they are really a kind of cash machine for the state, the state should be understanding of the sense of tyranny the cameras create.

It is time for the jackboot to come off the neck of the motorist. The Tories have been urging the government to see sense, and stop banning drivers who have only been exceeding the limits by small amounts.

I am delighted to see that the government has agreed, though it may come too late for me. We already have the most expensive fuel in Europe, now likely to rise higher. We have more and more speed bumps knocking off our exhausts.

If all this goes on, there will be a revolt on the roads, and I will be there, too, if only on my bicycle.

GOING MY WAY?

New research suggests that the cars we drive are a clear indicator of the way we will vote. So could changing your car change your politics? Boris was asked to climb into the opposition's driving seat to find out.

The trouble with campaigning in the wilds of Oxfordshire is that you lose touch with the main battle. I feel as if I'm lost in the jungle, way up the Nong river, 75 clicks beyond the Do Long bridge. We're fighting door to door, hand to hand. We think we are winning, but we are increasingly hazy, frankly, about events at the front.

So when my mobile went and it was some chap from the *Guardian*, I was thrilled. 'What's going on?' I bawled at the *Guardian* executive, because the reception is pretty poor in some parts of the Chilterns. 'Who's winning? How does it all look from where you are?'

'I haven't got a clue,' he replied. 'I am on holiday in Norfolk.'

'Then what do you want?'

'We want to give you a car,' he said. My mind raced. Why would the *Guardian* want to give me a car? It sounded like a stunt. It was.

As far as I could understand from my *Guardian* chum, there had been some kind of opinion poll – a totally valueless exercise, as we all know – about what kind of people drove what kind of car. It seemed that the typical Tory voter drove a Ferrari Testarossa or something, while the typical Labour voter drove a car called a Kia.

So the gag was to get a staunch Labourite to drive the Tory car, and to get me to drive the Kia.

'Do you get it?' the *G2* features supremo yelled from his Norfolk longboat. 'We want you to sit in that car and soak it up. We want you to imagine how it feels to be a typical Labour voter, on the principle that you are what you drive. What do you say?'

For a second I am ashamed to say that I almost said no. I was overcome by a sudden attack of pomposity. This was a serious business, this election, I thought. This was no time to be helping the *Guardian* fill its pages with droll wheezes.

And then I realised that of course it was really the *Guardian* that was helping me. It was going to equip the Henley and South Oxfordshire Conservative Association with a car and a free tank of petrol. It was a donation to our campaign! And when was the last time that the *Guardian*'s readers were identified with such a vital cause?

Good on you, *Guardian*! I said. Thank you, Scott Trust, thank you, Polly Toynbee, and mwah mwah. Send us the motor and I'll do you a review.

When the car arrived, I was so

pleasantly surprised that I began to doubt the entire basis of the wheeze. This is no Labour car. I have now been driving this Kia around for about five days and have discovered that it goes like the clappers.

The typical Tory voter drove a Ferrari Testarossa or something, while the typical Labour voter drove a car called a Kia.

OK, it is on the small side, but it has far more grunt than that dreadful Nissan Micra thing. It is nothing like as good as Oxfordshire's own Mini, but then I bet it costs much less, and it has completely Conservative road handling, cornering and all the rest of it.

A Labour car is some old Longbridge Austin Allegro with a broken sump and a pall of oil smoke coming out of the back. A Labour car is a new Rover, last pathetic relic of the British-owned volume car industry, felled by the incompetence of Stephen Byers.

This Kia is a Conservative car in at least two fundamental respects. It is like the Conservative vote, in that pundits tend to underestimate its size. You can easily fit five persons – 20 per cent more than you might predict, and in that respect I can confidently say that it will echo the Tory turnout on Thursday.

Above all, this car is deeply Conservative in the magnificent way it conserves fuel. Unlike Labour, it is thrifty, and economical, and sensible with taxpayers' money.

If ever there was a car that summed up the more-bang-for-your-buck-small-government Tory approach, it is the Kia. I don't know where these people get the impression that it's a Labour machine.

Wherever we go in its cheerful blue livery, we attract honks and waves. Labour? As we MPs say constantly these days, it's not what I'm hearing on the doorstep.

ACKNOWLEDGEMENTS

I would like to thank *GQ* for their kind permission to reproduce most of the articles in this book.

I also wish to thank the *Daily Telegraph* for their kind permission to reproduce the following articles:

  Motorists, revolt: me, I'm on my bike
  Going mobile

And the *Guardian* for their kind permission to reproduce the following:

  Going my way

ACKNOWLEDGEMENTS

PICTURE CREDITS

Alfa Romeo 156 Selespeed: © *Alfa Romeo.*
Lexus IS200: © *Lexus (GB) Ltd.*
Smart Car: *Martin Rose/GQ © The Condé Nast Publications Ltd.*
Range Rover Autobiography: *Tim Kavanagh/GQ © The Condé Nast Publications Ltd.*
Porsche Boxster: *Tim Kavanagh/GQ © The Condé Nast Publications Ltd.*
Jaguar XKR-R: *Tim Kavanagh/GQ © The Condé Nast Publications Ltd.*
MGF: *Tim Kavanagh/GQ © The Condé Nast Publications Ltd.*
AC Cobra: *Tim Kavanagh/GQ © The Condé Nast Publications Ltd.*
Chrysler Voyager: *Tim Kavanagh/GQ © The Condé Nast Publications Ltd.*
Delfino: *Tim Kavanagh/GQ © The Condé Nast Publications Ltd.*
Mercedes S55 AMG: *Tim Kavanagh/GQ © The Condé Nast Publications Ltd.*
Rolls-Royce Corniche: *Tim Kavanagh/GQ © The Condé Nast Publications Ltd.*
Chevrolet Camaro: *Tim Kavanagh/GQ © The Condé Nast Publications Ltd.*
Maserati 3200 GT: *Tim Kavanagh/GQ © The Condé Nast Publications Ltd.*
Porsche Carrera: *Tim Kavanagh/GQ © The Condé Nast Publications Ltd.*
BMW X5: *Tim Kavanagh/GQ © The Condé Nast Publications Ltd.*
Ferrari 456M: © *Ferrari SpA.*
Fiat Multipla: *Andy Fallon/GQ © The Condé Nast Publications Ltd.*
TVR Tamora: *Andy Fallon/GQ © The Condé Nast Publications Ltd.*
Mini Cooper S: *Piers North/GQ © The Condé Nast Publications Ltd.*
Jaguar X-type Sport: © *Jaguar Cars.*
Mercedes CLK500: © *Mercedes-Benz UK.*
Morgan Aero 8: © *Morgan Motor Company.*
Toyota Prius: © *Toyota (GB) plc.*
Porsche 911 TARGA: © *Porsche AG.*
Lotus Elise 111S: © *2004 Group Lotus.*
Noble M12 GTO-3R: © *Noble.*
Bentley Continental GT: *Simon Webb/GQ © The Condé Nast Publications Ltd.*
Mercedes SLK: *Armand Attard/GQ © The Condé Nast Publications Ltd.*
Nissan 350Z: *Armand Attard/GQ © The Condé Nast Publications Ltd.*
Lotus Exige S2: *Sara Barker/GQ © The Condé Nast Publications Ltd.*
Dodge Ram SRT-10: *Armand Attard/GQ © The Condé Nast Publications Ltd.*
Mercedes S500: *Simon Webb/GQ © The Condé Nast Publications Ltd.*
Ferrari F430: © *Ferrari SpA.*
Dutton Commander S2: *Armand Attard/GQ © The Condé Nast Publications Ltd.*
Caterham Seven: *Armand Attard/GQ © The Condé Nast Publications Ltd.*
Lamborghini Gallardo Spyder: *Will Whipple/GQ © The Condé Nast Publications Ltd.*
Armoured Range Rover: *Simon Webb/GQ © The Condé Nast Publications Ltd.*
G-Wiz: *Simon Webb/GQ © The Condé Nast Publications Ltd.*
Alfa Romeo Spider: *Simon Webb/GQ © The Condé Nast Publications Ltd.*
Boris Johnson on bike: © *Ian Jones/Telegraph Media Group 2006.*